# Did I Tell You This One?

William Flynn

FOR "DANNY BOY" GRIFFIN

# Preface

I've been telling stories for years about my career in the FBI as well as anything else I thought was interesting or might give people a laugh. Eventually I created a list in the notes app of my phone, just a sentence or a couple of words to remind me of each story. I would reference it from time to time when spending time with friends.

In September, 2022 I was in New Jersey celebrating my wife Linda's 75th birthday. During the trip I had the opportunity to visit some of my old FBI buddies at the Liberty Tavern in Union. Of course, we were telling stories among other things, when I mentioned my list. I scrolled through it and found a good one to share with the group and said; "Did I tell you this one?" My good friend Jim Ohlson quipped; "That's your book!"

Well, I'd never cared about writing an actual book. But I've always liked the idea of organizing the stories together somewhere -- in case someone might like reading them as much as I enjoy telling them.

A few years later my friend Daniel Reynolds was trying to help me retrieve some old photographs from a rundown computer I was getting ready to discard. He stumbled into a collection of my stories on the hard drive and really enjoyed them. He asked if he could help me arrange them into a book and I agreed.

"Do you have an idea for the title?" he inquired.

"Well, it's funny you should ask" I replied. "Did I tell you this one?"

# Roman Rocket

In 1978 Robert Daley wrote a book called "Prince of the City." Sidney Lumet adapted it into an unparalleled, motion picture masterpiece of authenticity a few years later. Treat Williams' portrayal of Detective Robert Leuci creates a cinematic experience that transcends mere storytelling; it's a visceral journey into the heart of moral complexity and human frailty.

Lumet's meticulous attention to detail, from the bustling streets to the smoke-filled rooms of the NYPD's Special Investigations Unit, transports viewers back in time, immersing them in the gritty reality of law enforcement in an era defined by corruption and compromise.

The movie resonated deep within me because it truly captured the flavor and atmosphere I experienced being a young, law enforcement person living in Manhattan during the 1970's. The detectives of the SIU were exceptional within the NYPD, navigating the complex web of corruption and morality.

In the heart of Manhattan, I lived the life of a single guy in his late twenties while tackling organized crime as an FBI Special Agent. My studio apartment on 75th Street and York Ave was more than just a place to crash—it was my personal oasis in the midst of the city's relentless energy, where I could unwind and recharge after diving deep into investigations and traversing through the urban jungle. I was a lucky guy. Just like the detectives of the SIU, I had a special job at a special time. There simply weren't a lot of other people who had a more interesting and exciting law enforcement career than mine. My apartment was located in Manhattan's exclusive Upper East Side neighborhood. The building was purposefully crafted as a studio building, prioritizing a fusion of practicality and comfort. The best feature of the apartment was the parking space that I had in the basement. Owning a car in Manhattan and navigating the notorious parking struggles makes the convenience of designated parking virtually invaluable.

The organized crime cases I worked were essentially Illegal Gambling and Shylock cases. They were a hot item in those days because they were big income providers for the mob and a source for assorted types of informants. I later went on to work some noteworthy union racketeering cases. However, the gambling / shylocking cases, also known as "loan sharking", were full of surveillances and interviews that were always unpredictable and interesting. The official name for shylocking cases was "Extortionate Credit Transactions", but we always called them shylocking cases. I suppose it might be politically incorrect today to use the term Shylock because the original Shylock was a Jewish money lender from Shakespeare's Merchant of Venice, hence it may be offensive to some. Get over it. Like I said, I worked Shylock cases.

The gambling cases were usually centered on wire taps of bookmakers who kept regular hours taking bets by manning phones in some seedy business location or in a marginal apartment where odd comings and goings wouldn't be noticed. The bookmaker would have to eventually meet up with his customers to settle up. We would follow them and identify the players. Later in an investigation you would approach these bettors to interview them

10

and put pressure on them to flip. It was important at the time and it was fun. I worked with other young agents and we were very contemporary guys whose unusual hours allowed us to hang out in the Eastside singles bars. We were hip; we were Princes of the City.

The Manhattan FBI office was located in an office building at 69th St. and 3rd Ave. This was about a ten or fifteen minute walk from my apartment and it couldn't be a better work circumstance. The neighborhood was a great neighborhood with mainly hi-rise apartment buildings with lots of street level stores, restaurants and bars. The non-surveillance suit and tie agents were easily spotted in the neighborhood and were welcomed by the locals for both their business and added security.

Manufacturers Hanover Bank was located directly across 3rd Ave from the office and this was a great convenience. ATM machines hadn't made an appearance yet so when I wanted cash, I would simply go across the street to the bank and cash a check. My partner at this time was my eternal friend Kenny Giel. Before we would take off for a day's work, Kenny and I would often go to the bank for a cash stop. This was always fun. We are both pretty outgoing but Kenny is an absolute showman when the circumstances are right. When we went into the bank we didn't just go in, we made an entrance. Everybody knew us and we were regularly greeted with verbal high fives from the employees. It was fun and the bank tellers liked us and we felt the same about them. The stand out was Ms. Linda Griffin. Linda was several years younger than me; tall, slender with the greatest head of wavy, long, auburn hair. She was Irish all the way with a million dollar smile but the thing that really jumped out were the most beautiful eyes I've ever seen in any woman. Linda was fun. Linda was a fox. We always kidded her and her girlfriend, Phyllis. Phyllis was a light skinned Black girl who was also very good looking. The two of them together on the street literally

11

had guys turning around to do double takes. They were the original Salt and Pepper.

On Friday nights Kenny and I would occasionally run into these girls and the rest of the bank people at the Sun Luck Restaurant that was located at 69th St. and Lexington Ave. We would meet my future Brother in Law Jack Maguire, who was a detective in the local precinct, and who was a virtual Mayor of the neighborhood. As the Crime Prevention Specialist he was in a Public Relations position with the PD and it was a perfect fit. This was also a hangout for FBI people who would have a couple of drinks before jumping on the subway to begin their commutes to the suburbs. The bank and the restaurant were all part of the Imperial House apartment complex that takes up the whole block. Linda's tales about Joan Crawford, the iconic actress turned recluse living in the Imperial House, were legendary. As Crawford's trusted confidante for handling her bank errands, Linda had firsthand insight into the mysterious star's private world. Despite her reclusive nature, Crawford treated Linda with respect and kindness, forging a unique bond between them.

Howard Cossel, the sports announcer, also lived in the Imperial House and every now and then would pass through the Sun Luck. We would chat about all sorts of things and buy the girls drinks. We were friends.

Joe Fanning was an old time agent that worked on my squad. He was a mentor to a lot of us young guys. We initially started out working a lot of his cases and the tradeoff was we got to watch how an old pro worked. Joe would come into work early and leave in the early afternoon to go to whatever horse track was running at the time. He kept an array of informants at the tracks and generated a lot of gambling case leads, as well as bunch of other work. Of course cigar chomping Joe played the ponies and was a Damon Runyon kind of guy who was meant to be at the track. This was his environment.

Joe's son Michael worked for a trainer at the Belmont Park Race Track and among his duties was the early morning timing of various horses' workouts. Michael got very adept at spotting up and coming future winning horses. Of course Michael would pass along this information to Joe who would bet on them and quite frankly, clean up. Joe was truly a good friend to all of us but for the guys who were willing to work directly for him he would quietly pass along the tips. We in turn would go to OTB (Off Track Betting) and place our bets. This was all perfectly legal. We did pretty well too. There was one point where Michael had given us 7 winners in a row. That was unheard of! When Joe called us it was like the EF Hutton commercial of the day, everyone listened.

It was a normal morning with Kenny and I at our desks catching up on whatever paper was due when Joe called. He told us not to bet the ranch on it but that he had one that looked pretty good. We lit up as we always did when one of these came in. Everything immediately was put aside and off we went to OTB. We needed a cash infusion for our bets so our first stop was Manufacturers Hanover of course. Our favorite teller Linda was working and as I gave her my check, I don't know why, I kiddingly asked her if she wanted us to place a bet for her. She asked me to put $2 on the horse and said that if she won she would take us to lunch. It's funny how my relationship with Linda was one of friendship and had been that way for a couple of years. I would see her at the Sun Luck on Friday nights every once in a while but I never asked her out. I have no idea why. As they say in today's language, she was "hot". Normally, if I thought I had a chance with a girl as good looking as Linda it didn't take me long to try my luck. The Sun Luck was always crowded but the bartenders Norman and Bob would save Linda and her girlfriend's seats at the bar. Linda served as the de facto private banker for the restaurant and they always treated her like a queen. I benefitted from her relationship with them because Linda was always able to get me a drink in this impossibly crowded bar. We were friends.

Michael's tip was a horse named "Roman Rocket". The horse came in but it only paid a whopping $2.80. He had extended his streak but there was no notable profit made. We won a little, but we certainly weren't complaining. We hadn't lost and we were looking forward to the next one. We told Linda about her questionable good fortune and she said that the lunch was still on. Of course there was no way we were going to let her pay.

The big day arrived and I was sitting at my desk as it was getting close to lunch time with Linda. I went to Kenny's desk to get us started heading over to the bank. Kenny sat back, looked at me and said; "Are you out of your mind?" He made it clear that he was not going to tag along on a date between Linda and I. Bingo, the light went on. This *was* a date with Linda, wasn't it? Somehow or another I had compartmentalized this get together as just a lunch with some friends.

I went across the street to the bank to pick up Linda for our date and she seemed to be under the same impression. It's incredible how quickly my attitude changed. I was looking at my friend with a whole new perspective. I was proud of the beautiful girl I had on my arm as we walked to Gleason's Bar on 1st Ave. This was a regular hang out of mine and one of a number that I frequented in my neighborhood. It was an Irish pub with a world class hamburger and it attracted a nice crowd from the famous Sloane Kettering hospital around the corner. We had a good lunch and it was never difficult keeping conversation going with Linda, it just flowed, everything was right.

During the meal, I sat facing the rear of the restaurant. I never did this and still don't. I'm like Wyatt Earp. I've got see who's coming and going out the front door. It was fortuitous that I deviated from my pattern because as I sat looking at the kitchen, a rat the size of your average house cat casually strolled across the floor. I almost pointed it out to Linda. This would have been a very critical mistake. As I found out later a roach would launch her, and so a rat would've likely required a 911 call. Strangely enough, as it turned out, it wasn't a bad omen. After that date, it just seemed to make sense that Linda and I would get together as much as we could. I got in the habit of picking her up with my car after work and driving her home to Inwood on the northern most tip of Manhattan.

We dated for a while and after some on again off again -- we settled in and got engaged. We started out broke, so we decided to have a small, immediate family wedding at our very good friends Judy and Bill Bradbury's home in Summit, New Jersey. At every turn, Bill "Boop" Bradbury expanded the guest list. Judy went with the flow and wound up doing a mountain of work with a great big smile. You have to have your cousins, your friends from work, and the friends from outside of work who you have known for years. Eventually, we wound up with about a 150 people in Boop's backyard with the most dangerous element you can have at any wedding, plenty of alcohol and no time limit. In a catering hall, they throw you out. We wound up with people sitting in the back yard at 4:00am. A clean up party started again at 8:00am and day two of the wedding effectively started. In the end, nobody got locked up, nobody got hurt and property damage was minimal. Thank God for small miracles.

Before we got married, I bought a house in Oradell, NJ, based on the strength of my good job and a flawless credit history. It was also based on my knowledge of the bank mortgage vetting procedures of the time. In other words, I borrowed the down payment for my home mortgage from the Federal Credit Union knowing that there was no cross checking between the two databases. To my mind, I knew that I could handle both payments and that my moral responsibility was to pay back my loans -- and I did. When Linda and I went to the closing in NJ we had just enough money to celebrate with 2 bottles of Michelob Lite, a bag of beer nuts, and the exact change for our return trip over the George Washington Bridge. Our life together got off to a great start, and we both feel we've been more than fortunate.

My single Prince of the City days came to an end but the tradeoff of finding my real Princess was a good deal. Who would've thought that Roman Rocket and a trip to OTB would equate to the most life changing event of my life?

# The Judge

I stood in the hallway outside of a federal courtroom in southern Manhattan as my partner Bill Bradbury was inside testifying. We were on an FBI surveillance squad at the time and were testifying to observations that we had made in an organized crime investigation. Honestly, I don't remember the specifics of the case but when Bill was finished he walked past me where I was standing in the hall with the court clerk and said; "It's a piece of cake, this guy's an asshole". He was talking about the defense attorney waiting for me to come in so he could trip me up and discredit my testimony.

I entered the courtroom and as usual, I was nervous and proceeded to the stand where I was immediately sworn in. No matter how often I testified, I always felt nervous. However, I also knew that once I heard my voice answering questions my nerves would settle down. The prosecutor proceeded to ask me about the observations I had made and it went as planned and he ended quickly. Up next was the abrasive hotshot defense attorney.

The famed councilor led off by violating a most basic rule of cross-examination; don't ask a question unless you have a pretty good idea of what the answer is going to be. "Agent Flynn before you came into the courtroom were you standing in the hallway waiting? Yes, sir, I was. Did Agent Bradbury pass you on his way out of the courtroom? Yes, he did. Did Agent Bradbury speak to you as he passed? Yes, he did sir." At this point, I can only speculate that Clarence Darrow thought he had me by the short hairs and that Bradbury was passing along some information to help my testimony which would be an obstruction charge at least. "And Agent Flynn what exactly did Agent Bradbury say to you?" I knew that I was at the Rubicon. I knew I was about to drop a bomb, and while stalling for a moment to make up my mind, I looked over at the Judge. He glanced at me and said, "Agent answer the question."

"Yes Sir, I will". "He said counselor that it was a piece of cake and that you were an asshole." The laughter was immediate and it was loud. I looked back at the judge and he was smiling. There were multiple defendants in this case and the guys laughing the loudest were the other defense attorneys. The defense attorney attempted to ask me another question but was rattled and stated no more questions. The judge told me I could step down.

I walked out into the hallway to exit and as I passed the Clerk of Court he smiled at me and said "Home run baby."

Did I tell you this one?

# Hard of Hearing

I went to a party one weekend afternoon at my sister Kathleen's apartment somewhere around Moshula Parkway in the Bronx. Ellen and Kathleen were just babies at the time and I brought along a friend of mine who I was working with at Lincoln Hall, Ron Logan. Lincoln Hall was a reform school run by the Christian Brothers where my brother Pat and I both worked and where Jack Flynn had also spent a summer or two. Ron was a big, charming, Irish guy whose mother lived on the Concourse. He blended into the family gathering with ease. Ron had recently returned from a trip to Ireland and was talking to my mother. Of course, Ron had no clue as to how hard of hearing Bridie Flynn was. "Mrs. Flynn, I never knew how many relatives I had in Ireland." To which he received the partially indignant response "Roaches? There aren't any roaches in Ireland." A pregnant pause ensued and the room broke out into laughter. Mom was great. She laughed at herself as hard as the rest of us did and I told the story on her for years. Bridie Flynn was a very good sport.

On another occasion, I was traveling with my beautiful wife Linda and my best friend Bill Bradbury from Charlotte, NC to our home in Emerald Isle,

NC. This was back when Bill and I were FBI Agents and we had all traveled to Charlotte on business. We stopped at a Boston Market to have some dinner. While the food counter had no customers when we walked in, there were plenty of people sitting at tables. Bill and Linda stopped to read the menu but I knew what I wanted so I proceeded to the other end of the counter to place an order. The counterman said something that I didn't catch to which I responded by saying "Am I lonely? How nice of you to ask." All of a sudden the entire restaurant broke out into laughter. Linda and Bill could hardly contain themselves. I looked around and strangers at the tables were laughing. Of course, I found out what the counterman had said was "Are you alone sir?" I started laughing myself. Yep, this hard-of-hearing thing is a Flynn family disorder.

# Franky Outdoors

Out on the North Fork of Long Island in Jamesport, New York is a famous restaurant named The Elbow Room. I frequented the place with my wife Linda in the late 1970s and as far as I know it is still there. It is famous for its marinated steaks and great cheeseburgers.

Its lesser-known, sister restaurant; "The Elbow Too" was located a little farther out on the North Fork in Laurel, a quiet hamlet. A guy named; Cliff owned the restaurants and his brother Franky ran The Elbow Too for him.

We frequented the "Too", as we started calling it among ourselves, with our close FBI friends the Abbotts and the Giels. Jimmy Abbott spent his summers growing up in the area and knew everyone and that included Franky. Jimmy and his brothers came up with the nickname Franky Outdoors because they maintained that they had never been there when Franky wasn't either behind the stick or sitting at the bar.

I remember going into the restaurant one afternoon with our usual crew and Franky was sitting at the bar with what I call a birdcage brace over his head that was anchored into his head. Naturally, we asked Franky what had happened and after some pinning down he confessed that he fractured his neck one night when he fell off a barstool. Somehow it seemed to be a natural accident for Franky to have.

While Franky was always there, the person who made the restaurant successful was his wife Ellen. Ellen was a waitress who took care of all the important things the restaurant needed. She was a great asset. Everybody loved her. She was organized and kept everything flowing.

My story begins one night when we were sitting at the end of the bar away from the kitchen waiting for a table. The place was packed. All of a sudden two cooks dressed in their kitchen whites came busting out of the swinging doors punching the proverbial shit out of one another. Ellen was standing right there and immediately got in the middle of the two brawlers. We stood up but there was nowhere to go. Franky had been standing directly in front of us behind the bar and motioned to go down towards the brawl. He stopped, came back, looked at us, and said; "On second thought, they probably won't hit Ellen."

As I said, Ellen took care of everything important at the "Too".

# The Man who died from Loneliness

Vincent suffered from two problems throughout his adult life, alcoholism and loneliness. The alcoholism started in the teen years and progressed throughout his life and while it was an issue that was always an ongoing battle, the loneliness was a hit-and-miss proposition. In the end, they came together and killed him.

At the AA meetings, everybody called him young Vincent because he looked ten years younger than he was. Vincent was just plain fun to be around; diminutive, neatly dressed, and a million-dollar smile. He first came around the meetings when he was 35 years old riding on a bicycle because his license was finally yanked for speeding. He was happy that it wasn't revoked for drinking because the speeding was only a six-month suspension while a drinking conviction could have been a suspension for 10 years. He looked like a 25-year-old kid on the bike, so when you found out his age it came as a shock. Vincent didn't exactly jump into sobriety with a clean leap. He was smoking pot for the first 6 months of meetings before he got the spirit and fessed up that while he had remained sober, he hadn't been clean. He hung in there and eventually got his license back, found a decent job, and got some good sober time under his belt.

While things were coming around in his life the one recurring theme that kept coming up as a problem for Vincent was this feeling of loneliness. He met women and dated but nothing ever seemed to come of it in the long run. One girl was older than he and already had a teenage child who lived with his father. She had her family, but Vincent wanted a family of his own.

Ultimately, the relationship ended and while it salved Vincent's loneliness in the short term, he felt that he was back where he had started. He was unique because he was the only man I ever met who felt that he had a biological time clock ticking. This is a phenomenon that is usually reserved for women but Vincent suffered from the anxieties that it produced. He wanted a family and the years were slipping away. This mindset resulted in his trying to make every relationship fit this mold and ultimately they all failed. His situation was further complicated by his physical living situation.

He lived in the same apartment that he had been born and raised in. When his parents moved out he took it over because it was rent-controlled and was an unbelievable bargain. This government rent control program wasn't meant to work this way and like so many programs, it had unintended consequences. In Vincent's case, the unintended consequence was that he felt that his life was passing him by and that he was trapped in this cage of an apartment but the economics of the situation forced him to stay. This was compounded by the fact that Vincent was a salesman who did most of his work from the apartment and often only left the apartment to attend AA meetings in the evening. He was stifled, both in his living circumstances and in his personal relationships circumstances.

Vincent often complained that for long periods he had no luck meeting any woman and that his only social outlet was the AA meetings that he attended regularly. In time the meetings became a problem as well because he started having relapses. While he would relapse, he always returned feeling disgusted and, as far as he was concerned, he was starting over. He felt that he lost his veteran status in AA when he relapsed and in a way he did. Ultimately, AA isn't about setting a record for the amount of time you remain sober, but rather about being sober to live your life outside AA. Some people who relapse during the AA program can turn the experience into a positive event by realizing their powerlessness over alcohol and subsequently redoubling their efforts to remain sober. Vincent took these relapses personally and to him they were scarlet letters that flagged him as a person of weak character, making each trip back to AA that much harder. As hard as his return trips to AA had become, Vincent's life was about to become a whole lot more difficult and to his great misfortune, dangerous. Vincent met Sofia.

As outgoing and likable as Vincent was during the periods of his sobriety when he was dry and content, Sofia was the opposite. Brooding and introspective, she didn't make friends easily so it took Vincent's gregariousness for them to have met. He had seen her on several occasions at the local supermarket. He had managed to strike up small conversations with her ending eventually with her agreeing to have dinner with him. Vincent was infatuated with her mysterious, slender, dark-haired aura. Her Russian heritage only added to the intrigue. They dated and slowly Vincent found out more and more about Sofia and the more and more intrigued he became. She lived with her mother, returning there from an abusive relationship with a multi-year boyfriend. She had finally extracted herself from this destructive circumstance and had started a new job as a flight

25

attendant resulting in her having an unusual work schedule. As far as Vincent was concerned, this added to Sofia's mystique.

Sofia was moody and mysterious and Vincent was entranced by her comings and goings. She kept strange hours, which were easily explainable by her employment, and it wasn't unusual for her to show up at Vincent's for a late-night visit. It became her custom to bring along some small, airline-size vodka bottles during her visits. Vincent of course didn't have any alcohol in his apartment and Sofia liked to have a couple of drinks, so what's the harm? The option of not drinking when she was around Vincent was unacceptable and Vincent felt he could deal with her drinking around him. Vincent was wrong. He started drinking with Sofia and in time Sofia moved in with him. This happened in a piecemeal manner, with Sofia leaving a change of clothes at the apartment initially and eventually after having a dispute with her mother, she moved in.

Vincent knew this was fraught with peril but his other nagging problem, loneliness, obscured his judgment. Although he stopped going to the AA meetings, he kept in touch with some of his AA friends and, in no uncertain terms, he was admonished that he was playing with fire, a very hot fire. His AA friends didn't know just how hot the fire was. The vodka bottles were the tip of Sofia's party iceberg, her real drug of choice was cocaine and her world was only right when everybody around her felt the same way.

Vincent was too smart to be oblivious to the serious trouble of continuing this relationship but his denial of the problem was significant. In time he became aware of Sofia's cocaine use and he dismissed it as best he could by going along with her line about it being a recreational thing and that it was a stress reliever from her pressure-filled job. Even though he kept up his phone contact with his AA buddies and they in turn told him that she either got help or got out, he just couldn't let go. He would get her help and she would change.  She was young.  She was beautiful.  She was the potential mother for the children he so badly wanted and most importantly, he wasn't lonely anymore.

His efforts to get Sofia into a rehabilitation center or to get her to some AA meetings went down a dead-end path.  She would stop drugs.  She would stop drinking.  What she really stopped was telling the truth about her drugging and drinking.  It became an often repeated drama of Sofia not coming home from work as expected and finally showing up with some lame excuse and then climbing into bed for extended sessions of sleep.  It went on for months with some periods of modest tranquility where Sofia appeared to be staying clean and sober.  Then she would relapse and promise to return to the straight and narrow only to relapse again.  Vincent at that time was doing the same thing only he confined himself to vodka.  He would console himself from the frustrations of dealing with Sofia's problems by indulging in his own major problem.   They were caught in a vicious circle, spiraling downward. Disaster was inevitable.

In time Vincent became disgusted with himself and with Sofia.  The blush faded from Sofia's rose and he ever so slowly started to see that not only was she a drug addict but that she probably didn't love him.  She would protest when he confronted her with these facts but he started to see that he was being used and in time he worked up a plan to put the relationship to an end.   Every year Vincent would go to Florida and visit his sister in Naples and over time he had made a small network of friends in the area.  He often had talked about relocating to the area and his profession as a salesman translated readily to finding work.  His insecurities in the past had prevented him from making the move. However, he finally decided to take the trip -- with the intention of a permanent move to the area. It was a "clean sweep", a new place to live, a new job, and a Sofia-free life.

Sofia discovered Vincent's plans when she saw some notes he had made about airline reservations lying near his phone and she confronted him at the first opportunity. At first, he told her it was a vacation and she knew he was lying because he would have used her free tickets option available through her job. She persisted and Vincent told her the truth. He had had it and he wanted out. She needed help and wouldn't get it. He too needed help and was going to do just that. They wrangled, fought, and carried on for days about the trip but Vincent was adamant. He was going to Florida and restarting his life. He assumed she didn't love him since she refused to get help. Sofia pleaded that she indeed loved him and that she too wanted a new start and they could do this together. She made a compelling argument that she could easily transfer with the airline and that this was just what they needed to get their lives together back on track. They would get straight and sober together, get married, and have the family that Vincent so badly wanted. Sofia struck a chord in Vincent's heart and he couldn't resist. She convinced him that this would be a storybook ending to all their problems and he eventually gave in and plans were made to go to Florida.

Vincent's sister Laura was very surprised when two deputies from the Sheriff's Office knocked on her door one fateful Saturday morning. She didn't realize it but she was being given special treatment because she was a friend of the Sheriff from the golf club to which they both belonged. Normally she would have received a phone call asking her to come to the office but it was certainly better handled this way. Sofia found Vincent dead that morning on the living room sofa, in the condominium where they were staying and the police had been summoned. While they were not positive of the circumstances of his death until the autopsy was completed, the paramedics at the scene believed that he choked to death on a piece of food and that the physical setting in the living room indicated that he had probably been drinking at the time. Laura was stunned but deep down inside this terrible news didn't come to her with the impact that most of us have felt when someone we love and are very close to dies unexpectedly. She knew Vincent was in trouble and she just plain did not like Sofia who she saw quite clearly as someone who was using him to continue her drug-addicted existence.

Laura's friendship with the Sheriff came into play a second time when she sat down and talked to the female deputy who interviewed Laura at the condominium on the morning when Vincent's body had been discovered. At this point, the results of the autopsy had been received and it was confirmed that indeed Vincent had choked on a piece of food and that his alcohol blood level was well over the legally drunk limit. Laura also found out that some of the furniture in the apartment had been overturned and that the detective conjectured that Vincent must have done this to summon help as he realized he was choking to death. When the call came to 911 for assistance from Sophia, the autopsy determined that Vincent had already been dead for five or six hours. At this point, the detective confided in Laura that she became quite skeptical of Sofia and her explanation as to why she didn't hear the commotion that Vincent must have made. Sofia claimed she had gone to bed, exhausted from a day spent laying around the beach and going to a late lunch. The detective further told Laura that she suspected from her observations of Sofia and Sofia's defensiveness about the whole evening in general that Sofia was a drug addict and that she was most probably in a drug-induced stupor when Vincent was dying. Laura provided information to the detective about all the things that Vincent had told her over time and confirmed the conclusion that the detective had arrived at.

As it turned out, there was nothing to be done regarding Vincent's death from a police point of view. There was no foul play and while it was most probably true that Sofia was under the influence of an illegal substance when Vincent died, nothing could be proven so the investigation was closed as an accidental death. Laura of course agonized that had Sofia not been doing drugs maybe she could have helped Vincent and this was very upsetting to her.  In time, however, she realized that Vincent had made his own choices regarding Sofia. She also learned that Vincent had been drunk when he died -- another poor decision.

  In the end, alcohol played a significant role in Vincent's demise, but the true underlying cause of his death -- was loneliness. Vincent was the man who died from loneliness.

*Did I tell you this one?*

# The Tannery

I was visiting Ireland with my wife Linda and our good friends Ken and
Sue Giel. We separated from a larger group and were headed to Cork to see
my niece Christina Healy. We only had two days before we had to be back
in Dublin and spent the first night in Dungarvan, County Waterford. I need
to explain that my mother was from nearby Cappoquin in Waterford and I
have many first cousins who reside in the area. As a boy of 12, I spent a
summer on my uncle's farm and visited Dungarvan several times. One of
the visits was to a county fair and I had never been so close to a large array
of farm animals and products. It made a life-long impression on me.

We stayed at a B and B where the proprietor was kind enough to make
reservations at a restaurant for us called The Tannery. She made the
reservations in my name, Bill Flynn. The Tannery it turns out was a five-star
restaurant owned by a renowned chef named Paul Flynn. It was an actual
tannery down by the wharf in town that was converted to a restaurant and
had an unusual layout. As it turned out it was very fine dining. We arrived
and were seated in short order when the owner came over to introduce
himself and have a chat. He saw my name on the reservation which of

course was the same as his and led me to explain about my mother being from Waterford and my father from the adjoining county Cork. We determined that we were not likely related and we really enjoyed the evening and chatting with Paul Flynn.

The next day we drove to Cork where we visited my niece Christina at her home near Blarney Castle. When we walked in she greeted me in her beautiful Irish brogue; "And sure Uncle Bill, how was the Tannery last night?" Needless to say, I was *very* surprised to hear her question. "Christina, Ireland is a small country but it's not that small."

Christina went on to explain that the girl who waited on our table was Una Ahearn, my first cousin Tom Ahearn's daughter. She overheard our conversation with Paul Flynn and surmised that it might be me. What cemented it for her was that I resembled my older brother Greg Flynn. He's a lifelong African missionary who stopped in Ireland every year and who she already knew.

The Ahearns reached out to Christina to confirm if, in fact, I was in Ireland. I was beyond embarrassed. Because of my limited time, I decided not to contact any relatives. I didn't want to visit with one of them for a few hours and risk the chance of slighting another. To this day, I don't know if Tom Ahearn was slighted. I suspect not. He's not that kind of person. What I will never understand is why Una didn't introduce herself. It must be an Irish thing. I can't imagine any of my American nieces not getting fully engaged in a similar situation. Oh yeah, the first thing I asked Kenny was "How was the tip?" "No problem, good to go." After all, that might have been the most important thing.

# Gil Kelly

Gil Kelly was like any other kid growing up in the Bronx in the fifties. Every day was exciting. There were dozens of friends to play with and all it took was going downstairs and looking around the block or going up to the corner to find them. If that failed you could go and call for one of your friends and see if they could come out and play. There were no car-pools or for that matter for most kids, no cars. Just get out of the house and find your friends and everything else took care of itself. Play centered around the basics. We played with balls of all kinds, roller skates, jump ropes, and bicycles. There were no Playstations, Gameboys, computers, or iphones; we just had each other and the basics. If you didn't have the basics you could go to the park where the "Parkie" would lend you a basketball, a softball and bat, a knock hockey set, chess, checkers, or some other game in exchange for anything as security. A Police Athletic League (PAL) identification card, a shirt, a hat, a bottle of soda, almost anything worked as security. Gil loved all these things just as much as any other kid but there was another side of him that was entrepreneurial and it surfaced even this early in his life.

Every Saturday during the summer in the PS 115 schoolyard the competition would begin. There were several Korean War Veterans who would meet, and choose sides and the stickball games would begin. These games would last all day and they were serious business. There were four or five guys on a side and the games were for money. Probably a dollar a guy a game but whatever the amount was it was serious money to the participants. Since this kind of money was at risk, the equipment had to be first class. The bats were the standard broom handles and each player had a preference but the balls were the most crucial and there was only one that would do, the Spaulding. It was pronounced "Spaldeen" and they cost twenty-five cents apiece. There was a competing ball called a Pennsylvania "Pinky" but you would rather play the game naked than be caught using a "Pinky". The players would chip in and start the game with four or five balls. Inevitably, during the day balls would be hit over the school roof or they would split from the tough use they got. This would call for a run to the candy store for replacement balls. Enter on to the scene, Gil Kelly. Gil would always volunteer to make the run and these guys meant "run" to the store. There could be no delay tolerated in getting the new "Spaldeens" and Gil would never disappoint them. Gil of course was looking for a tip but this couldn't be counted upon so he further volunteered to make other candy store runs to get Cokes and Pepsis. The charge for this service was a two-cent deposit on the returned soda bottles. Typically by the end of play, the overall winners would give Gil a quarter tip and this combined with his deposit money was a pretty good deal for a young kid. This was Gil's first venture into the world of moneymaking and while he loved getting the money, it wasn't predictable and steady. Gil decided that what he really needed was a job and it wasn't long before he found one. This job, while it was his first, taught Gil as much about life as any job he would ever have.

Gary Jacobs was an entrepreneur with several vending machine routes that he had established around the Bronx. He had a wife and two young kids and an itch to move to Pearl River, NY and that took income. His vending machines were a source of the best kind of income, cash, the unreportable income. He had peanut machines, gumball machines, trinkets in plastic bubbles machines, and best of all -- stamp machines. The stamp machines were a necessity for most candy stores and drug stores. They were draws. The merchants wanted to provide the stamps for their customers who were usually too far away to get them from the post office and once in the store, they would pick up their cigarettes, newspapers, coffee, and any of a dozen other items. Gary purchased the stamps from the Post Office and then added on 30 to 50 percent depending on the type of postage. The stamps were good profit and they were an easy sell to the merchants. He could then piggyback his other machines into the location and everybody made money and life was good.

The peanut, gumball, and trinket machines were easy to deal with. All Gary had to do was go to the stops to top them off when they needed to be re-supplied and collect his money. The stamp machines were more complicated. The stamps were dispensed in white cardboard packets that had to be carefully loaded into the machines and the packets had to be loaded with the stamps. This job was a labor-intensive proposition and it required someone who would work for cheap. Enter Gil Kelly.

Gil heard about this job from Jimmy O'Mara who had just quit to move on to a Bronx Home News Route. Jimmy told Gil that you had to be fifteen to get the job but if you told Gary you were fourteen and would be fifteen in a month you could get the job. Gil was thirteen but he was big and he went with Jimmy to meet Gary where he was prepared to lie to get the job. It didn't really matter what Gil said. He was getting hired and Gary went through the charade of asking his age. What mattered was what Gary was

35

going to pay Gil and that was a flat fee of ten dollars for all the stamps that had to be "stuffed" which amounted to about a dozen trays. It was a daunting task for an adult much less a thirteen-year-old boy but Gil was eager and excited. He told Gil that he would let him into his shop on Tiebout Ave. at 7:00am on Saturday morning and Gil was expected to stay there until he finished the stuffing.

Gil was excited and his first Saturday was a training session where Gary both taught and assisted him in getting the stamps stuffed. Between the two of them, it took them eight hours and this was a long day for the young boy but it was tolerable. His enthusiasm for his first real job and a crisp new ten-dollar bill never allowed Gil to think ahead to the next week when this task would be his alone.

Gil showed up promptly and Gary got him started, then left and a very long day ensued. The shop itself was not conducive to doing anything comfortably. Gary was a slob with boxes of trinkets and peanuts stacked everywhere. His desk was overrun with invoices and paperwork that spilled onto the dusty, dirty old wooden floor. The bathroom in the back was an old toilet that even a thirteen-year-old boy knew was a health hazard. These conditions were augmented by the pervading stench of cat urine. In the midst of this, Gary bred Siamese cats that he kept in cages immediately behind the desk that he provided for Gil to do his work. Gil knew he didn't like this environment but it didn't occur to him to complain. This must be the way people work in real jobs. To add insult to injury, Gary asked Gil to leave him a note if he heard the cats making any loud screams because this would indicate that they had mated. Gil liked this least.

Gil began his work enthusiastically cutting sheets of stamps into strips that would then be stacked and stuffed into strips of the still-attached white cardboard packets. The packets ended up in bundles of ten after they had been separated at their perforation lines. These bundles were wrapped in rubber bands and stacked in the trays that Gary ultimately took to the stores where he filled the stamp machines. The process is difficult to describe but what is important to note is that it took a certain amount of physical dexterity to accomplish and this of course would only be learned over time. One Saturday's work was not a long enough period to learn this skill and the day stretched into a fourteen-hour ordeal for the young Gilbert. He had gotten discouraged during the day but he had taken the ten-dollar bill that had been waiting for him when he showed up at work. A weary Gil had finished his work and a life lesson had begun.

Over the next month, Gil was faithful to his job and he stuck with it although he thought about quitting several times. He liked that ten dollars and he liked the notoriety that having a job brought to him. His manual skill at the job had increased significantly and he was now getting the work done in ten hours but it was still far too long a day as far as he was concerned. Gil didn't like going to the shop, which was still a rat hole, and it didn't even have a radio. He had asked Gary if he could get him a radio and Gary had responded that he would see what he could do. Gary did nothing and resentment was starting to build in the young Gil. It took him another two weeks but Gil conjured up the courage to ask Gary for a raise. Gary's response was predictable; he would see what he could do.

Gary never brought the subject up. Eventually, Gil confronted him very timidly. He had rehearsed exactly what he was going to tell Gary many times. Gil pointed out that Gary had told him he was doing a good job. He told him that he had gotten as fast as he was going to get at the job; and that it was taking him ten hours. And that he felt he deserved to get a raise. Gary had obviously thought about the raise issue as well. He explained to Gil that when he started the job it took him fourteen hours and that since he was getting ten dollars for the job, this translated to seventy-one cents an hour. Now that Gil was doing the work in ten hours he was making a dollar an hour. Gary told him he had already gotten a twenty-nine cent per hour raise. Gil didn't know what to say and said nothing. He knew that he still wanted more money. He knew that he still hated coming into the same filthy shop. He knew that Gary had never gotten him the radio that he had asked for but he was at a loss for words. He knew that he felt unrewarded for the effort that he had made to become skillful at what he did and he knew that his resentment was getting bigger by the minute.

Gary had made six stops before lunch on Monday and in his usual fashion, he called home to check with his wife to see if there were any messages. Debbie, Gary's wife, told him she was glad that he had finally called. The phone was ringing off the hook. Retailers were calling and they were not happy with the complaints that they were getting from their customers. It seems that the stamp machine packets were either missing stamps or were packed with stamps of the wrong denomination. It took a while for it all to sink in with Gary. He started retracing his steps and after examining several of the machines, he could see clearly that this was not a random happening. This was no simple mistake but rather a flat-out sabotage. Gary had to go back to each store, retrieve the packets to make sure that they were all in the same condition, and then call all his other stops to let them know that he wouldn't be able to stock their machines that day. What had happened to the boy Gil? He must have known what he was doing. Why had this happened? It wasn't long before Gary had his answer.

Gary parked out in front of the shop and when he went inside he didn't notice the usual stench of the cats. He had long ago accustomed himself to the odor because to him it ultimately was the smell of money. He also didn't notice the smell because he was angry, very angry with the boy, Gil. He would have gone to find him but he didn't know where he lived. He knew the boy lived on Ryer Ave. somewhere but that was all he knew. The family didn't have a phone and that wasn't that unusual in this neighborhood. Gary also knew that these Irish kids came from large extended families with older brothers, uncles, and fathers. You had to be careful in how you dealt with them and deep down he knew he really didn't want to find him He went to the old wooden desk and he took out the thin flimsy desk key and opened the big side drawer where he kept his stamps. Gary was going to have to spend the night re-packing all the cardboard packets and then spend a very long next day straightening out all the stops. Sitting on top of the stamps was a piece of lined note paper that looked like it had been torn out of a child's black and white marbled cover notebook. Gary realized that the paper must have been slipped through the drawer front crack along with a crisp fresh ten-dollar bill. It slowly started to register with Gary as he perused the note. He reflected on Gil's several requests for a raise. He remembered the boy asking him a couple of times about getting a radio and he knew that Gil particularly did not like having anything to do with the cats. The note now all made sense. Written in the imperfect scrawl of a thirteen-year-old were the simple words   "I'm returning the ten dollars. I didn't do the work. You should have treated me fair. Now you know how I feel." --Gil.

Gary surprised himself with his long-term reaction to what he started calling the "stamp caper". The initial anger subsided and no small reason for this was the fact that Gary knew he had screwed the kid. The kid was entitled to some small raise and was a radio such a big deal? He was like a madman initially but after he calmed down his wife talked some sense into him. Eventually, he came to appreciate the "balls" that the kid displayed by getting even with him. It took a long time but Gary eventually turned the "stamp caper" into a self-deprecating story that he told himself at different get-togethers. Gil Kelly told the same story for years to come but his version had nothing to do with self-deprecation.

# Phil Mickelson

I've always enjoyed upbeat, positive stories about famous people. They are generally all the better when they come from a personal source and not just from the public record. Here is a cute one I have about the legendary golfer; Phil Mickelson. If you're a golf fan you probably have good vibes about Mickelson. He has a natural humility about him and his gambling style of play makes him very, very popular.

I know a young couple who live at the Muirfield Golf Club in Ohio which is the Jack Nicklaus course where the big-time Memorial Golf Tournament is played every year. They reside in one of the more modest homes and have two lovely daughters. The girls were 8 and 10 years old when the big tournament took place a few years ago. They set up a lemonade stand along a part of the golf path where each golfer would eventually walk by. Sure enough, Phil Mickelson came by and stopped at the stand. He asked the girls how much the lemonade cost and they told him it was a dollar per glass. Phill said great and ordered a glass. The girls served it up and Phil gave them a bill and told them to keep the change.

Later on, the girls excitedly ran inside to show their mother that Phil Mickelson had given them a $10 bill and told them to keep the change. Mom checked it out and said; "No girls, that was a $100 bill."

Doesn't it make you smile to hear this little vignette? There it is. A private act by a public figure simply to put a smile on the faces of a couple of little girls. This story always cheers me up and I hope it did the same for you.

## Vincent and Vera

Throughout Vincent's life, he loved music. He had a popular music brain that knew thousands of songs and the artists that performed them. When he was a boy doing his homework in the corner of a bedroom in a wretchedly small apartment in the Bronx he always had a radio turned on. It was ever so low so that his mother wouldn't be alerted and in retrospect, he never did remember her complaining about it to him. I guess Mom was just glad Vincent was doing his homework quietly. She had six other kids to keep honed in on and when Vincent got near that radio he was never a bother. Vincent, as a boy then and an aging man now, always had to know the name of the artist performing any particular song that caught his attention. He had called radio stations on several occasions to find out who sang a particular song and was always pleasantly surprised that he had never been turned down for an answer. He remembered when Elvis Presley appeared on the scene with Blue Suede Shoes and Hound Dog. Who was this guy? Was this guy Black? He had never heard anything quite like this singer but it was Heartbreak Hotel with its echo chamber sound and its lovelorn lyrics that got his attention. Vincent was to become a lifelong fan of the King. Some other groups and songs had made lasting impressions on him. The echo chamber sound of There Goes My Baby by the Drifters with its first use of violins in a Rock and Roll song compelled Vincent to always find out who these people were.   He knew silly arcane songs like Sheb Wooley and The Purple People Eater, and beautiful instrumentals like Santo and Johnnie's Sleepwalk.  Vincent's brain was an encyclopedia of artists and songs and it was because of this that when it happened he knew he had a problem, a very serious problem.

   He had been sitting at a light in his car when Heartbreak Hotel was played on an oldies station and was a novelty.  Of course, Elvis got lots of play on the radio but not usually Heartbreak Hotel. The oldies playlists are rote items that are virtually indistinguishable around the country from one city to another.  You would often hear "Are You Lonesome Tonight", "Jailhouse Rock" or "Love Me Tender" -- but not "Heartbreak Hotel".  Vincent had often complained about the oldies lists to his other music-lover friends and he was always evaluating the songs when he listened to the radio.  When Heartbreak Hotel came on the radio it got his attention, it was a departure from the norm.  There it was "If your baby leaves you and you need a new place to dwell, just take a walk down "lonely street" to Heartbreak Hotel. It'll make you so lonely baby, it'll make you so lonely, you could die."  It was followed by the staccato guitar lick that he could recognize in three notes.  He knew the song, but for a brief moment, he couldn't remember that Elvis was the singer.  This wasn't like trying to remember some remote fact like "where did the Chantels of "Maybe" fame" get their name from? St.Vincent De Chantel parish in the Bronx by the way is the answer for you lovers of useless information.   No Vincent not being able to remember that it was Elvis was the equivalent of not being able to remember his own name. He couldn't rationalize Elvis.  This was like not recognizing his own face in the mirror.

Vera loved Vincent. She met him in a bar in Manhattan that they both frequented after work and she knew she had a potential keeper when he didn't try to bed her down on the first date. He was very respectful of letting sex take whatever amount of time it would take for Vera to be comfortable with it. That didn't stop him from kidding her about it while still being a very romantic guy. He had managed to turn some awkward moments into fun times. She was impressed with his knowledge of music. He would find songs on jukeboxes when they went dancing and tell her all about the songs before he played them for her. He knew the lyrics and the sentiments of so many songs and they just had lots of old-fashioned fun whenever they went out. He was a good guy and Vera recognized this and in short-order they loved each other and they married. It can honestly be said that neither Vincent nor Vera regretted a moment of their lives together. It was because of this love that Vera was concerned for Vincent. He had become forgetful and while he was in his mid-sixties, that was young by today's standards. She noticed that he seemed disoriented about things that should not have been any kind of a problem. They were at a dance in the community center where they lived in Florida and Carla Thomas sang out over the speakers "Gee Whiz look at his eyes, Gee Whiz how they hypnotize, He's got everything a girl could want, man oh man what a prize." These were lyrics that he used to kid her with, claiming that Vera knew that these lyrics had to have been written about him and yet when they played he seemed to draw a blank. Something was wrong and Vera was afraid to bring it up. It had the potential to be the most terrifying thing that would ever happen to them.

Vincent's love was music and Vera's was the computer. She had been exposed to the cyber world early on when she was working and she ultimately became a Net Head. It was her tool of first choice when she wanted information and it was with considerable trepidation that she went into her Google search engine and typed in the word that she dreaded most,

45

Alzheimer's. After perusing a couple of websites she had a thumbnail sketch of symptoms for victims of this most debilitating of diseases. Forgetfulness, irritability, personality changes were just some things to watch for and Vincent was evidencing all the things that she read about. Her research indicated that as the disease became more advanced it displayed progressive irreversible memory loss. Apathy, speech and gait disturbance accompanied by disorientation would take from a few months to four or five years to set in with a complete loss of intellectual function being the final outcome of the disease. When Vera turned away from the computer she experienced for the first time a tension in her stomach that would become a normal part of her life. She knew deep down inside that Vincent had the dreadful disease but what she didn't know was that Vincent's suffering was going to be matched by hers.

The worst day of Vincent's life was upon him and he knew it when he sat waiting in his car for a light to turn green. For the third time, Vincent could not remember why he was in his car or where he was going. He just followed the traffic and eventually, it dawned on him where he was and how to get home. When he was clear-headed again, he knew that he had had another episode of complete forgetfulness and all he could think to himself was that he was losing his mind. Vincent had never been this frightened before and he had to confide in Vera that this was happening. She would know what to do and how to handle it. Deep down inside, the voice that we all use to talk to ourselves with, told Vincent that this was the beginning of a very long end.

Vincent was sitting in his old easy chair listening to Don And Phil Everly beautifully harmonizing "Let It Be Me" with its opening lyric of "I bless the day I found her" when he decided that this was the right time to tell Vera all about what was happening to him.  It turned out to be a short conversation with Vera because both of them were so afraid and Vera told him that she was already aware of his episodes. She held his hand and told him she loved him and that they would go to the doctor. They could do so much today with drugs and they could prolong the onset of serious forgetfulness. Vera knew the word dementia but she couldn't use it and they never said "Alzheimer's" in one another's presence.

As time passed, Vincent's world became smaller and he knew what awaited him. When he had his rational moments, he remembered all that had happened to his best friend's Father and their family when he was diagnosed with Alzheimer's disease. The everlong slide into dementia was coupled with anger and personality change. Vincent was most afraid of all the anger that he had inside of him taking over and exhibiting itself on what amounted to the strangers in whose hands he would inevitably be left. He listened to Bonnie Raitt with her "Just In The Nick Of Time" sing about a friend of hers who was "scared to run out of time". Vincent saw this as his dilemma. He was "scared" to run out of rational time.

Vera had the support of her wonderful girlfriends to fall back on but watching Vincent slide away into an unknown world was the worst thing that had ever happened to her. He could still be left alone for short periods, even when his dementia had set in, and thank god there were still times when he knew what was going on. Mainly he had to be reassured that she had enough money to get on with after he was gone and he constantly told her that he loved her and that without her he wouldn't have had the great life that he had. He had become sedentary at this point and although he certainly had the predicted anger, it was always directed somewhere else. She knew that she was losing Vincent even though his body was still in her presence but she always kept an image of the vibrant man that she had spent her life with and this allowed her to carry on respecting him fully.

Roger Miler sang "One dying and a burying, some crying, six carrying me, I want to be free". Vincent wanted to be free. Certainly, he didn't want to face the ordeal he had already begun to experience. More so, he couldn't bear the thought that Vera would have to watch him shrivel up into a fetal-positioned cadaver that happened to still be breathing. All the while he would drain her resources leaving her at the mercy of the government programs. Vincent's choices had narrowed down and time was not on his side.

The police jumped when the dispatcher announced that there was a report of shots fired at a residence on the shore road. This simply did not happen, shots were not fired in this middle-class tourist town and they reacted by approaching the residence when they arrived with their weapons drawn carefully down by their sides. A woman ran from an adjoining house when she saw the police and explained that she and her neighbor Vera, who was visiting, heard a shot come from Vera's house and called the police. Vera was in the woman's house too terrified to come out and see what had happened. When the police entered they found a dead man sitting in an old recliner easy chair, which had been covered with a large beach towel. The man was bleeding from his temple and a Smith & Wesson 9mm automatic pistol was lying on the ground about 6 feet from the chair. It was later determined that the gun had been fired once by the man. He had gunpowder traces on his right hand and the kick of the pistol when it was fired had flung it from his hand to where it had landed on the garage floor. The police had discovered two envelopes at the crime scene. The first envelope was prominently placed sitting on the hood of the man's Jeep Cherokee and the note inside was not addressed to anyone. It simply stated that indeed what had happened here was a suicide and that there was no foul play involved. The second envelope was addressed to Vera and sat on the dead man's lap.

The funeral arrangements had been made and members of the family and several close friends had come to town to see Vincent off. It was a sad time for everybody but a couple of Vincent's old friends talked among themselves away from the family. What would you have done if you were in his shoes? Could you have done the same? Was it a coward's way out? They discussed it and all the old theoretical arguments that they used to have about the sanctity of life seemed to fade away. There was no real condemnation of Vincent but one pointed out that Vincent had been an ardent anti-abortionist and wasn't this at the very least an inconsistency? Another pointed out that abortion was all about the taking of innocent life and that Vincent's act was, it seemed to him, in some way both courageous and a crime at the same time. In the end, they all agreed that Vincent had been a good and decent man and that if forgiveness existed in eternity, it would be there for Vincent.

Vera was every bit the distraught widow when the funeral finally got underway. She felt that her reason for living had come to an end but she knew that life always kept moving forward. She would have no choice but to do the same. Everything was painful for her but the thing that bothered her most was the feeling of relief that she felt inside. She was guilt-ridden with this thought but she couldn't deny to herself that she honestly believed that it was better this way. In her hand, she clutched the letter that she had gotten from the police and she had read the few lines a dozen times already. "Vera. Time is running out for me. I am rational now and this is the most difficult thing that I have ever done. Forgive me. Please don't think me a coward for nothing could be harder. Pray for me and know that I have done this for both of us. No one has loved anyone more than I love you. Vincent"

As the coffin was wheeled down the aisle towards the rear of the church the only music to be heard that day began to play. Amazing Grace had begun, sung by the King, of course.

# Marty O'Dea

I grew up with Marty O'Dea in the Bronx. Marty was a couple of years younger than me and he was a roly-poly kind of kid who hung around with his friend Quinn. They were ball players who were always on the street or in the park participating in whatever sport the season allowed. Stickball, touch football, handball whatever but it was basketball that dominated and was played year-round. They lived on the basketball court.

I lost track of Marty but he grew up to be a 6'4" monster of a guy. He had acquired the demeanor of someone you simply did not screw with. He played basketball at Iona College for a while and I know he was a bouncer at a popular singles bar near Parkchester in the east Bronx. It was the era of bar fights. The fights were always fist-fights. No guns. No knives. No weapons. With Marty around, the fights were fewer and very short. You just didn't push it with him.

Marty, while a tough guy was also a man of good character and he wound up in the Port Authority Police Department for New York City. Port Authority cops are the people you see around the airports, tunnels, and bridges. It was on the George Washington Bridge one afternoon as Marty traveled to work that my story begins.

The traffic was at its usual bumper-to-bumper snarl. Someone in a Mercedes' behind Marty blew his horn. In those days the Mercedes cars had loud obnoxious European horns and this made it even more annoying. The third horn blast did it. What did this moron think was going to happen by blowing his horn? Were the cars going to miraculously open up and a path would clear? Not a chance but what it did do was to get Marty out of his car where he walked back to the car's driver-side window. He badged the driver and motioned him to roll down the window. It took a moment but Marty recognized the driver. It was Skitch Henderson, the band leader for the Johnny Carson TV show who was a well-known personality at that time. Marty acknowledged that he was surprised to see Henderson and they passed some pleasantries with Marty asking some questions about Carson. It was a generally civil chat with Marty explaining that the traffic was situation normal. He buttoned up the conversation and started to walk away. He stopped paused turned around walked back and said, "Oh Yeah, by the way, BLOW THAT HORN ONE MORE FUCKING TIME!" Up went the window.

Marty went back to his car. Mission accomplished. There was no more horn-blowing. And good ole' Skitch Henderson had a fun little story to pass along to Johnny Carson that evening.

*Did I tell you this one?*

# Fat Albie

Six of us left the FBI office on 69th Street and headed to the Nassau County Court House in Westbury, Long Island. We took three cars and we were going out to arrest Fat Albie Roma. It had been determined that Albie had a court appearance and since we had a warrant everything seemed to fit. There was the only hitch, our illustrious supervisor thought it would be a good idea to follow him around all day before we arrested him. It would be useful to know who some of Albie's victims were but usually an arrest warrant means forthwith and since Albie had been among the missing, why fool around. In short, the troops were not happy with this idea and it was a bad way to start the day.

Fat Albie was of course fat. At 5' 6", when you tip the scales at 275lbs. you fit the label. Albie was not a Lou Costello kind of fat guy however, he was a wide-shouldered bull of a guy who scared a lot of his organized crime compatriots. He was also a truly mirthless man. He saw no humor in life and he didn't like people. Albie brought to this assembly of attributes another feature that made for a deadly mix, he was mean. The thing that got Albie out of bed in the morning and motivated him to keep on the move most of the day was his uncomplicated love of money. This combination of character traits lined up very nicely for Albie in this life because his chosen profession was that of a shylock. Albie lent money out at usurious rates. If Albie gave you $1000, at the end of a week you owed him $2000. If one of his customers couldn't pay, he kept Albie off his back by paying the interest, the vigorous ("vig") on the debt. To collect these wonderful returns on your money you often have to go to some extremes and it is helpful to be an Albie kind of guy to get the job done.

You have to wonder why anyone in their right mind would get mixed up with a guy like Albie. The answer isn't really that complicated. The people who get involved with the Albie's of this world are people who are as screwed up as Albie but in a different way. Enter Gerry Dane. Gerry Dane was a frenetic personality who had a hard time literally staying still. He had a quick mind that was very good with numbers and this served him well in his chosen profession as a middle school math teacher on Long Island. Gerry didn't really like teaching but rather he liked the time off it provided him. As a math teacher, his syllabus repeated itself, for the most part, year after year and to sum it up, Gerry could do this job in his sleep.

Gerry had one trait that mirrored Albie and that was his passionate love of the quick buck. The free time that Gerry achieved by being a teacher was fully occupied with his consuming addiction to gambling. Gamblers and borderline businessmen, these were the stock and trade of Albie Roma's customers and there seemed to be an inexhaustible supply. The businessmen borrowed the money because their legitimate credit was either bad or exhausted and they usually had some kind of a payment that they were waiting on. Albie was the solution to a short-term cash flow problem and most of these people paid Albie and we never heard from them. The gamblers were a horse of a different color, literally.

Andy's story is both compelling and illustrative of the complexities of addiction. His life, marked by a whirlwind of highs and lows, reveals how each addiction manifests uniquely, but none so insidiously as gambling.

Andy, a charismatic mailman from Patterson, New Jersey, was known for his outgoing nature and wild lifestyle. Over the years, he grappled with multiple addictions—marijuana, cocaine, heroin, alcohol, and a surprising sexual addiction. His charm wasn't limited to his job; he knew everyone on his route and had a following of lonely, overweight women who appreciated his attention, no matter how fleeting. His dual life involved keeping a balance between his work, his vices, and the thrill of his risky behavior. Yet, despite his ability to juggle all these aspects of his life, he found gambling to be the most challenging addiction to overcome.

Andy's insight into his addiction struggles reveals a lot about the nature of gambling versus other forms of dependency. With substances like drugs and alcohol, the effects are glaringly visible. The physical toll is apparent—you see it in your reflection, feel it in your body, and it's impossible to ignore. The visible decline provides a harsh reality check, making the struggle with substance abuse painfully evident, even when denial is strong.

Gambling, however, is different. Andy described how, unlike the external evidence of substance abuse, gambling's impact is less visible. You maintain an outward appearance of normalcy, going to work and interacting with family, while internally, you're caught in a relentless cycle of hope and despair. The thrill of the gamble and the promise of a big win keep the cycle spinning. Each relapse is driven by the belief that the next time will be the breakthrough, that big win that will solve all problems. Yet, this elusive jackpot often never comes, and even if it did, the addiction to risk and the chase would pull you back into the cycle.

For Andy, gambling's allure wasn't just about the money but the constant need for excitement and risk. Unlike other addictions, where physical deterioration is a visible consequence, gambling allows you to keep up appearances while slowly destroying your life from within. The constant pursuit of the next big win and the thrill of the gamble become all-consuming, making recovery particularly arduous.

Andy's reflections on his battle with gambling versus his other addictions highlight the unique and often hidden nature of gambling addiction. His experience underscores how gambling can operate subtly, often masquerading as a seemingly manageable aspect of life, while it secretly wreaks havoc. His story serves as a reminder of the multifaceted nature of addiction and the different ways it can ensnare individuals, making the path to recovery a complex and deeply personal journey.

Gerry Dane was always looking for the right selection. He was both a sports bettor and a horseplayer and his string was well run out with his bookmaker who was making threatening calls to his wife at her job. She flipped and Gerry made the jump to the ultimate problem solver, Albie Roma. This match was quite suitable for Albie because Gerry was a weasel and Albie knew that it wouldn't take much to get Gerry to bleed his wife and relatives to pay him off. Of course, Gerry got behind on his payments right away and Albie had him meet him in a restaurant to straighten out the problem. Gerry thought he was going to pacify Albie with a bullshit story which was always his response when the walls closed in but not this time. Albie listened to his spiel for a short while and responded by letting himself slip into a controlled rage as was his technique for putting the pressure on and the meal ended up with Albie jabbing Gerry in the eye with a shrimp fork. Albie gave Gerry one week to come up with his "vig" payment or Gerry was getting his head broken.

Gerry panicked and now showed up at the FBI's door looking like Captain Hook and portraying himself as a righteously wronged citizen. His story started out as a business venture that had gone bad and his newly acquired partner Mr. Roma had assaulted him.

It didn't take long to get the real story out of Gerry and the work of getting some evidence on Fat Albie began. Gerry, who was basically a spineless human being, needed a lot of motivation to make the taped phone calls that are usually the first step in this kind of investigation. His propensity to bullshit everyone around him however took center stage and Gerry pulled off the phone calls with some skill. Gerry got Albie on the phone and with some newfound bravado supplied by our presence, he told Albie that he would have to wait for his money and that he had more pressing obligations. Albie bit -- hook, line, and sinker. He cascaded Gerry with every obscenity imaginable, and his controlled rage ended up with his telling Gerry that he would "Kill him and his family" if he didn't get his money. "Fuck with me and you're a dead man!" It was exactly what we needed, a death threat. He demanded a meeting the next night and we were thrilled to oblige.

The meeting was set for 7PM in the parking lot of a pizza joint in Levittown, Long Island and since it was during January it would be dark at that time. This worked out OK for us because it made it easier to set up for surveillance yet there was enough ambient light for photographs. We secreted a body recorder and a transmitter on Gerry for the meeting and had him arrive in his auto just before the meeting time. This was no easy feat because of Gerry's total lack of physical courage. Some victims enjoyed telling the shylock to stick it knowing that they had us to back them up but Gerry wasn't one of them. He was extremely nervous and as it turned out he should have been. Gerry arrived at the pizza place at 7:00 pm as planned but Albie was not prompt. We used this time to check our radios and to get set up for photos. Gerry had a Nagra tape recorder on his person and this was the machine that we used exclusively in the 70s when these events took place. It was very dependable but you never know what you have on tape until you play it back. The transmitter, which provided the live coverage of the event, was another story. We always had problems with these items and they would broadcast intermittently for absolutely no discernable reason. The lead surveillance unit would monitor the transmitter and relay commands to the other units on another radio. All the units could monitor the transmitter on a handheld radio as well and this is what they usually did. Albie was fifteen minutes late at one point and Gerry was under strict orders not to leave unless one of us walked by him and told him to. We waited a while and eventually he arrived.

Albie showed and things went along much as we expected with him threatening to dismember Gerry and his kids if he didn't get his money. Shylocks talk real tough but the last thing they want to do is kill you. They want their money and about as far as they will go is usually a good roughing up to get your attention. If they're feeling particularly benevolent, they will threaten to go to your place pf work and let it be known about your gambling and your debts. However, they know that dead people don't pay. Most of the conversation took place in front of the pizza place, and at one point Albie grabbed Gerry and pulled him into the alley alongside the shop. Of course, at this point, the transmitter starts cutting in and out and while we saw Albie slap Gerry in the head we could hear Gerry telling us intermittently that he was being murdered by him. Now I know that you expect me to tell you that we jumped out of our cars and arrested Albie, but that isn't exactly the way it worked.

We were presented with a dilemma. Of course, we had our observations of what happened as evidence but we didn't know what we had on tape or photos at this point. We knew that the transmitter was scratchy and our tape of it confirmed that later. If Gerry could walk away from this work we would have the time to analyze our evidence and to follow Albie around for a while to line up his other victims for testimony against him. Our decision was to let it ride and to see how far this went. Of course, we didn't tell Gerry this beforehand or he would never have shown up. Albie slapped him again so one of the agents was sent to walk by the alley and to stop and to yell at them questioning what was going on. Albie told him to stick it but it did the trick. It scared him into letting Gerry go with the understanding that they would meet in three days that Gerry was expected to have sold his car by then and that Albie would get paid in full.

We retrieved Gerry who was upset that the cavalry hadn't arrived and soothed him by telling him that we had witnessed the scuffle, my choice of words, and that everything was going to be fine. Gerry's version was that he had been brutally beaten and that we had screwed him. Of course, when we insisted that we take him to a hospital to check out his life-threatening injuries he cooled off. He admitted that he was a little melodramatic and when we appealed to his almost non-existent macho side we had him feeling like he was a real ballsy guy who had stood up to a badass. The whimpering on tape was conveniently forgotten. Gerry however was now totally useless in terms of meeting with Albie and honestly, I must confess that I would have felt the same way. We lucked out with a good tape and decent photos. By not arresting Abie on the spot, we gained a couple of days to see if we could find more victims. However, Albie had already more than incriminated himself, an arrest warrant was obtained and we found ourselves in Westbury, Long Island.

My partner Bill Bradbury and I were instructed to go into the courtroom to take Albie out on foot and put him in a car. A team of units would follow him for the day and arrest him that evening after seeing who he met with. Yeah, right. There were about a dozen people in the court room of which we were two and it took Albie maybe ten minutes before he became

Did I tell you this one?

suspicious of us. His hearing was continued and we followed him out to the parking lot alongside the building where he promptly disappeared. Great. We notified the units of his disappearance and a grid of the area to spot him ensued. The area had already been swept around the courthouse to find the car he usually drove but that had turned up negative. After half an hour of fruitless search, the teams split up and headed out to known hangouts looking for the fat man. Boop and I stayed in the area in case Albie had been picked up by someone and perhaps had to then be dropped off later to pick up an unfamiliar vehicle that he may have driven to the courthouse. While we waited, Boop and I expanded the grid, and to our surprise, we found a car that was the same model as Albie's but the license plate was one digit off. We ran the plate and it came up registered to a female who was unknown to us. This was too much of a coincidence for us so we set up on the vehicle. We didn't know what we had so we didn't call back the other units. It turned out later that our unknown female was a girlfriend of Albies and they had matching cars with vanity plates that were separated by one digit. Albie was a romantic and Boop wondered if they wore matching pajamas as well.

We agents who worked the ECT violation in those days also worked Federal Illegal Gambling Business violations and it was always your aim to generate informants. A guy like Albie was in a position to provide valuable information about gambling operations and when you had him in a bind like this, you always let it be known that a deal was a possibility. We threw this out on the way to New York but Albie wasn't biting. Boop was trying to be Albies' best friend but no matter what kind of small talk he generated, Albie was playing it hard ass all the way. We arrived in New York and took Albie up to a small interview room on the sixth floor which was normal procedure. He was fingerprinted and photographed and an inventory of his personal effects was then conducted. These items would be secured in an envelope and ultimately turned over to the marshal's downtown after Albie's arraignment. Boop was going through the items and it was a normal collection of pocket gear that people would have on them. He had a wallet with a license and an assortment of credit cards as well as some business cards. There were also car keys on a ring with a mini flashlight and a comb. What was not so normal, but when you think about it not too surprising, was a great big fat roll of cash.

Boop went through the items recording them on a form that Albie would ultimately sign and be given a copy of. He was making a production out of this and I was asking myself why he wasn't in a hurry. Albie was a dead end and the sooner we got him through the process, the sooner we were free. He counted out the money and stacked it in neat piles. $3,500 in $50's and $20's were laid out on the table. Boop picked up the piles one by one and made one large roll. He neatened up the roll by tapping it on the table much like you would with a deck of cards. He then folded it in half and put it in his pocket. He leaned over the table, looked our boy Roma dead in the eyes, and said; "Albie, you can go home now." Albie hesitated and said; "Are you kidding?" There was a pregnant pause before I said "What do you think?" Albie leaned back in his chair, looked back and forth between the two of us, and responded; "I think you're jerking me off". It was spontaneous. The three of us started laughing uproariously and the tension was finally broken.

Albie ended up serving a couple years in prison for this. Then, about 10 years later he got what he had coming. I remember reading about his dismembered body being found in the trunk of a car somewhere in the Catskill Mountains. The case was never solved. Gerry Dane, who was a very young man when all this occurred, is still out there teaching our grandchildren about statistics and odds. How poetic.

# Manhattan College

I began attending Manhattan College in 1962 and got out on parole in 1969. Rudolf Giuliani, the famed Mayor of New York City, and James Patterson, the famed novelist were in attendance at the same time. I didn't know them of course. They were students. I was an attendee. I was totally unprepared for the independence and responsibility that college life offered. I was a successful high school student in a structured environment but a disaster on my own in my first semester of Liberal Arts with a 21-credit load.

I literally struggled for several years, just squeaking by, and eventually was about to be thrown out when my older brother Bro. Greg Flynn, a member of the Christian Brother's Order who ran the College, interceded and got me an interview with Bro Francis the Dean of the evening Business School. It was a short interview. Bro Francis was a gentleman and he simply stated "Son, this is the last train. Make the most of it."

I drove a school bus during the day and worked as a waiter on the weekends. However, I still found time to go partying while I neglected my schoolwork. That was about to come to an abrupt change. During my first evening class, I found myself seated next to John Brennan, a guy I graduated with from Good Shepherd Grammar School in Inwood, Manhattan. What a pleasant surprise. John was a nice guy and he told me that he lived across the street from the school with his wife and child. I was floored. I didn't know guys my age who were married with a child. John had a full-time job during the day and was getting his degree at night. He wasn't the only one in class like this. There were several family guys of varying ages and when it came to school, they were dead serious.

It took several years but being in the presence of serious students had gotten me to the point where I had finally graduated. So I thought. I went to my senior advisor to get final approval on my courses and was shocked when I found out that I didn't have a required theology course. We discussed it and it was determined that I should go and see the Dean and request a waiver. This had to happen.

Brother Francis was long gone and a layman, Mr. Chambers had taken his place. He was a pleasant man and of course, I had seen him around the halls over several years. I made an appointment and went to see him one evening. I was nervous. A lot was riding on his decision. I had a job waiting for me upon graduation. I proceeded nervously to explain my plight and as I pushed forward with my request he stopped me. "Wait a minute, are you saying you're a student here. I thought you were a teaching assistant. You've been here longer than me." I told him my request quickly and he waved his hand to give him the request. He quickly signed it. "If for nothing more than persistence Flynn, you deserve to be on your way." He shook my hand and wished me well.

I will always be grateful to Bro. Francis and Mr. Chambers and thanks to them, I too like Giuliani and Patterson before me, am a graduate of Manhattan College.

# The Old Man

The old man sat looking out the window of his room. His view overlooked part of the parking lot where the dumpster collection area was tucked neatly into one corner. The saving grace of the view was the one section of green lawn and a single cluster of trees that attracted a lot of bird activity. The well-worn leather chair that he sat in was comfortable and he didn't have to crane his neck to see the view. All in all, he had no complaints. He was a frail man who moved slowly when he went for his walks, but he was steady on his feet. He had the aches and creaks of old age but he was content because he slept well again and for the most part felt rested. His truly closest friends and relatives had all passed and at times he felt very alone. The hardest part of coming to the close of his life; was the fact that nobody was around who understood what his time on earth had been all about.

The pretty young woman, the friendly volunteer from church, came closest to understanding and that was only really a guess on his part. She was a lovely girl, a good listener who asked an occasional question and, as best he could tell, seemed to understand the huge difference that he felt from the young people in the world that she inhabited. Another hard part of his great age was having this feeling of possessing some unique wisdom that only his long life experience could provide and that no one was interested in hearing about it.  He commanded respect from his friends and peers based on the strength of his character, personality, and insights.  In his world now, it was only his personality that counted.  He had understood throughout his life that politeness and civility were the glue that kept society away from each other's throats and this served him well now.  He had witnessed his beloved mother achieve a great age with the minimum of complaints and with gratefulness to her creator for all the good that her life had.  As she had taught him in life, he was following her death example.  The workers in the facility around him were appreciative of this positive attitude and responded with friendliness.  He was grateful but inside, he felt it wasn't enough.

He understood that hardship and even abuse early in life could be turned around into positive forces if the person involved understood this.  Mistreatment can toughen the frail and make wise the naïve if someone can point this out to them when they are suffering and exhort them to turn negative events into a positive.  The extreme poverty of his youth had made him wise regarding the acquisition of wealth throughout his life.  His parents forced frugality taught him a respect for material things and he never took his success in life for granted.  He was quite human and he had squandered money on foolishness and often on the search for good times in his youth but the basic lesson was well grounded and ultimately he always returned to the deep-seated values.  He regretted that he hadn't seen the wisdom of sharing his wealth with the deserving poor earlier in his life.  While he was generous by nature, his greatest admiration was for those who were able to either share what they had or live a religious life and work uncompensated for what they did.

The old man felt particularly sorry for the silver spooners that he had met in his life who had inherited a privileged life and who never had the blessing of having experienced deprivation.  They had nothing to compare their comfortable lives to and for the most part, took their good fortune for granted. He believed if a person could start at the bottom and work and strive for something in life, how very sweet was the taste of success when it arrived? Not all the privileged took their wealth for granted and he had witnessed up close the lives of several in this position who were kind, generous, and understood that their good fortune was an accident of birth. Others however were fixated on material things and were often unreasonably demanding of people who would come into their sphere of influence. They seemed to believe that if you did not match their wealth, you were ultimately just another form of "the help". Other silver-spooners reveled in their good fortune and saw their birthright as a mandate to increase their wealth and god help those who got in the way.

Many of the children of his generation had the great burden of having to overcome a privileged existence and based on what he saw in their lives, as far as he was concerned, they had failed. They embraced divorce quite comfortably and shattered families with dysfunctional children had become a norm rather than an exception. Many were godless and lived their lives for self-indulgence, a concept he just didn't understand. There isn't enough paper to explain how he felt about those who supported abortion. He considered it to be the ultimate scourge on all society but this generation seemed quite comfortable with it and this was their most damning indictment of all.

He was an environmentalist long before it became the only religion that many in the society now proclaimed. He wasn't comfortable wasting resources. When he performed his morning lavations, he turned the water off and on rather than just letting it run. He never understood paper towels when the cloth was just plain better. The over-packaging of all goods in the society of this day was obscene to him and in later years when he went to the supermarket, he brought along his canvas bag. There were countless

66

numbers of simple things that he did in his life of this nature but his aggravation was great for the showboat environmentalists. These were the once-a-year Earth Day crowd who showed up a Central Park for a rally and left hundreds of tons of litter behind them while they indulged themselves in the rantings of vegetarian, sun-worshipping, Wiccans. There was much he had to say but there was no one to listen.

The dining room was a chore for the old man and he tried to have his meals sent to his room but the nurses were having none of it. They all agreed that the interaction with the other residents was an important event for his mental health and well-being. On the contrary, the old man knew that every meal was a depressing experience for him. He felt particularly bad for the residents who were just hanging on with little or no idea of where they were and who were being fed like children. Certainly, there was no benefit for them to be fed in a community setting but the staff bought into this community concept big time and there was no talking them out of it. He suspected that it was easier for the staff to do it this way but on the whole, they were decent people and he wasn't about to hurt their feelings by speaking his mind. He tried to make the best of it at first and engaged some of the residents in conversation but they all turned into complaint sessions. Now he was able to cut his meals short by going for a walk immediately afterward which was the only thing that the staff encouraged more than community meals. .

As he gazed out the window of his room for countless hours his thoughts almost always returned to the friends that departed and to the wife of 50+ years whom he had dearly loved. He had understood that as his friends had passed away, the only way to deal with death was to continue in life with even more attention to its wonder. In concentrating on the countless simple beauties and goodness that existed in the world for those who chose to see, he was able to overcome the grief of the loss of the ones he loved most. He lived life to the fullest so he could honor those who had died. It was different however when his wife died, very, very different.

She had suffered from heart disease and while it had limited her activities, she had not suffered any great pain from it. She passed away in her sleep and really it wasn't unexpected but when it did happen, it still came as a shock. He was truly devastated but the long-range emotion that he felt was that of sorrow for himself. Logically, he understood that her life, judged by anyone's standard, was good and caring and that if there were peace in death she would have it. What he felt overwhelmingly was sorrow for himself.

Would he ever see his beautiful girl again? It amazed him that while she had aged most gracefully he never saw an old woman when he looked at her. He always saw the beautiful waving brunette hair and the big green eyes that surrounded the biggest, brightest smile. He loved to observe her and her interactions with all her girlfriends. The way they made endless social engagements and were able to get excited about all of them was a constant fascination to him. He loved the way she was able to feel sorry for anyone needing help and then figure out a way to help them. But what he admired and loved most about her was her ability to overcome the accidental death of her only child. She suffered greatly for years but in the end, she did not allow it to sour her on life. No, she made the most of other people's children and had a profound effect on how well they would lead their lives. It was this thought that eventually allowed him to become comfortable with her death and to accept the circumstances that he was in.

The old man knew quite clearly that he was at the end of his life and his thoughts turned to the most important and the least discussed subject of his life, God. What was it about this subject that had made it so hard for him and his friends, even him and his wife to discuss? Was it a feeling of unsophistication in admitting that you believed in God that kept people from speaking about the subject? He wasn't really sure what all the others whom he had loved believed nor was he sure about that which they may have been skeptical. He would never know. They were all gone. His thoughts on the subject however were clear and for the most part remarkably simple. Was there a god? He came down resoundingly in the positive. The awe of creation that he felt throughout his life always led him to a belief in God. Particularly, those times when he was alone with a sky filled with stars, a vastness too large to imagine, did his reason cry out for a belief in a creator. Why had every culture of man that ever existed acknowledged a deity? Was it not a part of the human makeup to at the very least arrive at the question of a god? These things alone, he felt, should at least make one wonder.

He saw that all the things around him had a beginning, middle, and end. Why would this not apply to the very universe in which we all live? Didn't we have to suspend our logical thought processes to believe that from no creator at all came the very world in which we lived? Was it always there? Didn't it have to have a beginning and if so, a creator? Was he to believe that from nothing, a series of chemical actions perhaps, ultimately came the world in which he lived? Did he owe his very existence itself to such a cold and secular event? Not hardly.

The old man wondered about the eternal, more ethereal values that existed in this world. Where did love, beauty, justice, kindness, truth, and all the other wonderful eternal values come from? Did they spring from the mind of man? Are they chemically caused emotions that are useful for the survival of a species? No, he believed they stood alone, on their own as another part of creation, and further confirmed his belief in the existence of God.

For the old man, the hard part of determining how he would live his life came when he confronted the issue of Christianity. He had accepted God but could he accept the concept that God had sent his son to earth in the form of Jesus and that the true road to salvation came through the acceptance of this dogma? Some Christians believed that their religion was the only road to Salvation. So did some Muslims. There were probably other major religions with believers that felt that same way and if so, who was right? The old man concluded that none of them were right. His logical mind told him that all religions evolved from a need by man to satisfy his innate belief in a creator and that charismatic figures came along and capitalized on this need. He didn't question their motives for he believed that they were probably benevolent. He knew that Christian believers would tell him that the acceptance of Jesus was a matter of faith and that this was the crux of the entire belief system. What was he to do? Should he suspend his logical common sense insights and adopt this Christian belief system or should he go it alone and live his life as he saw fit?

The old man had struggled with this issue because it wasn't as simple as his mind had first made it appear. He had been raised as a Catholic and he had a great respect for the people and the institution that he had known as a boy and a young man. He had fallen away from this church not because he had questioned its basic beliefs but rather simply because he had begun to live a more hedonistic lifestyle. He was going to have a good time and that didn't include a church-going lifestyle. He didn't delude himself. He had just drifted away and he made no excuses. Over the years, he had heard former Catholics attribute their exit from the church to reasons that ranged from corporal punishment in school to pedophilic priests. They would often state that more people were killed in the name of religion than anything else and therefore implied that they were better off for not following any religion. Of course, they neglected to see that the secular states under Mao, Stalin, and Hitler probably had the highest body counts of all. He doubted that they had had any real questioning in their minds when they left but probably had done the same thing as he had but just chose to place blame elsewhere. In time he had come to understand that there was a need in this world for good people to follow a conscious moral path and to make no excuses for attempting to do so. He could not live his life haphazardly relying on his belief in God as his only yardstick. If everyone followed this precept, moral chaos would follow. While the Catholic Church was as flawed as any other church or for that matter any other institution of man, it did present to him a basic set of beliefs that he felt were moral and honorable. It exhorted people to love one another and to treat each other in a brotherly and sisterly caring fashion. He knew that enccylopediactic volumes could be written to show where it failed but, the core beliefs were worth pursuing and he believed it necessary in some way for salvation. The eternal value of justice demanded that those who lived their lives abusing others would ultimately have to be punished and if not on this earth, then where? No, salvation was not something that he could ignore; it was real and something that had to be addressed.

There was a quiet stirring in the corridor of the home with some of the staff quickly scurrying about to attend to another deceased resident. It seemed to the old man that their strategy was to remove the resident quickly before it became too upsetting to the others in the home. They didn't understand that it wasn't that upsetting. Every one of the alert residents knew that the home was the last stop and that their turn to be carried out would come. They almost universally accepted that others around them would die soon and had built up unconscious defenses to deal with these events. The people who dealt the best with these deaths however were the people of faith. They believed that they would find everlasting peace and forgiveness for their sins. The old man was jealous of those who had true faith which he came to see was the greatest blessing of all. He had resolved many years before to return to church and he again returned to prayer. He had always believed in prayer and prayer had worked for him. When he was courting his wife he had stopped into a church and knelt and prayed to God to allow the relationship to work because he loved the woman. He believed that she would be good for him and shortly thereafter the relationship turned around and blossomed into marriage. His prayers since he returned to church were simple and consistent. He prayed that everyone ultimately might find peace and he prayed that he might find true faith. It hadn't happened in all the years he had now gone to church but he understood that it was far better to have lived a life trying to follow the tenets of Christianity than to have simply ignored it.

In the end, his attempt to find faith and the belief that something good awaited people who tried to live moral lives brought him much comfort. He didn't find unquestionable faith but he did find a lessening fear of death. He wanted to see what was on the other side. The most comforting thought of all was his belief that in some fashion, in some way that he could probably not conceive of, he would once again be with his beautiful girl.

# The Grim Reaper

Bill Bradbury was my very close friend from the early 1970s when I met him in the New York Office of the FBI where we were Special Agents. Bill was from Chicago and had the pleasant personality that many mid-westerners are blessed with. I'm safe in saying that Bill Bradbury didn't have an enemy in this world and I can also add, that he probably never met anyone who didn't like him. Having said that, the thing that bonded our friendship was a dark humor streak that Bill had that only surfaced with people he knew really well. I used to kid him and tell him if these people knew what you were thinking about they'd be amazed.

Case in point; when I retired in 1998 I was diagnosed with prostate cancer. I knew it was coming. Over time, my father and three brothers all had prostate cancer. I also knew that I wasn't going to fool around with any of the alternate treatment options available at that time and that I was going to have my prostate removed. I had confidence in my doctor and that was his recommendation as well and we set a date for the operation.

My good buddy Bill came to visit me before the operation and he bought a greeting card with him. Honestly, what man brings a card with him when he comes to visit another man? Bradbury did and here's why. The card he gave me had a picture of the Grim Reaper on the front. It was ominous with the black hooded reaper and his staff staring glumly at you. When you opened the card there was the reaper again staring at you with a finger waving you closer saying "THAT'S RIGHT, COME TO PAPA."

I laughed of course. It was hilarious and fit his real humor to a tee. I went in and had a successful operation and you might think that this is the end of my story. It isn't. Years later Bill had an operation to deal with and it weighed on him because he was a hypochondriac. I went to visit Bill several times before his operation but the last time I brought him a greeting card. My wife Linda found the perfect card. She had actually come across the card earlier on but instinctively knew she had to buy it. The front of the card was the picture of a rear-view mirror in a car and in the mirror was none other than a menacing Grim Reaper leering at you. When you opened the card it read, CAUTION: IMAGES IN THE MIRROR MAY BE CLOSER THAN YOU THINK.

Sadly, Bill passed away in 2014 and I can't think of him without smiling. He met the Grim Reaper, as we all will, and I'll lay money on it, that the Reaper liked him.

# The Rescue

Everything happened so quickly. There was an explosion that sounded like it came from the belly of the ferry and the next thing that the man knew; he was floating in the water. There had been no time to think, just react and he had immediately jumped in the water and started swimming away for fear of another explosion. The ferry had been closing in on the terminal when it happened and the people who had been waiting for the ferry's arrival were turned into would-be rescuers. The man found himself fighting a current that was pulling him and several other people away from the ferry dock. He found that he was able to make progress against the current, which was gentle, but he was afraid that it might pick up. The people at the dock were yelling at him and the others and they were holding up a lifesaver and a rope. He quickly understood that they wanted him to get into range so that they could toss this out and start pulling people out of the water. He yelled to the other two people who were near him and they indicated that they saw the people on shore as well and they all were proceeding towards the dock.

It was at this point that he saw the golden retriever dog paddling along about 15 yards to his left. The dog seemed to be responding to calls that he heard from the shore and was headed in that direction as well. The three people and the dog were all abreast of each other and they had about a hundred yards of water to cover to get in reach of the rescuers and their lifesaver. The man was pacing himself and he felt that while he initially made good progress the current was making it harder as he got closer to the shore. The other two people were well behind him but the dog was still abreast of him. He was unable to worry about the others, it was getting to survival time and that was all he could think about.

Finally, he was able to get himself to the point where the rescuers were able to throw the lifeline to him. The dog was still about 15 yards to his left and didn't seem to be able to make any more progress than he had been able to. The first toss missed him and fell between him and the dog. The rescuers were shouting but he couldn't understand them. They pulled the lifesaver back and re-tossed it but this time it was closer to the dog than it was to him. He was about twenty yards away from them but still, he felt that they should have been able to get it closer. They retrieved it and tried again. It landed even closer to the dog. He was truly frustrated and redoubled his effort to paddle closer to the ferry dock. As he got closer he could hear some of the calls of the rescuers. "O'Malley, O'Malley", he thought he heard them yelling. That wasn't his name. Were they yelling at the other people? Not likely, they were out of range behind him. They tossed the lifesaver another time and it almost hit the dog on the head. "O'Malley, O'Malley", again they were calling.

It hit him like a hammer. He was getting very tired, not exhausted. He still had strength and it was from this strength that he drew his anger. It

76

became apparent that the rescuers were calling to the dog. They must have known this animal and O'Malley must have been the dog's name. It all made sense in an instant. It was fashionable with many yuppies to name their pedigree dogs with an Irish Sir name. He had encountered it many times. These people must have been meeting the ferry when the accident occurred and realized that this was the dog of the person that they were meeting. Again another toss of the lifesaver and again it was to the dog. The man could feel the adrenalin pumping in his veins. He would swim to the shore. He would make it. He would see the people who chose to save a dog over a human being.

## Harry and Roberta

It didn't come as a shock to Harry Tromberg when the doctor pronounced his cancer death sentence.  He'd been sick for a year with assorted ailments and repeated trips to various doctors had not been able to diagnose his problem. Finally, an oncologist with a new cat scan had seen what everybody else had missed -- pancreatic cancer. Harry's parents had both died relatively young from cancer and he already lost a brother to the disease as well. He was a realist about his health but he was also a pessimist by nature. He usually saw his glass as being half empty and when the bad news was delivered it just seemed natural to him. Still, the pronouncement had that shocking effect that we have all experienced when we receive a jolt of bad news. Even if it is expected, when you hear the actual delivery, you ask yourself; "Is this really happening?"  It didn't help that Harry was a walking medical dictionary and he knew as much about pancreatic cancer as probably any other laymen in the country. He knew it was surely fatal and that it would be a very unpleasant way to die.

The news of the cancer was only the first of Harry's problems brought on by the doctor's pronouncement. The other problem he had was his wife

Roberta. Roberta had been at Harry's side through his myriad trips to the doctor and the two were not dealing well with the strain that this brought on. Quite frankly, they had a loveless marriage. Prior to Harry getting sick, Roberta had told several friends that she was leaving Harry and going to live with her daughter. Harry didn't know Roberta had told people this but he did know that the marriage was in serious trouble and that Roberta was not someone he could rely on. They were both in their second marriages and had children from their first. Harry had an adult son and daughter. Sandra was a beautiful young woman who was engaged to an impressive young man and they both had professional careers. His son Matthew was a doctor in training and was beginning his residency along with his lovely girlfriend. Harry was quite proud of both of them. He had custody of his children and raised them as a single parent -- and had done a very fine job. Roberta was equally devoted to her daughter Cindy, who was a very successful High School Senior and who was the only person that Roberta loved more than herself.

Roberta found herself in a strange position. Harry was going to die but he had an insurance policy worth $750,000. He had complete legal control of the policy, and if Roberta was going to get her share -- she would have to hold his hand while he died. Harry was a controlling man in the best of circumstances and in his dealing with death he was going to be at his most demanding. Roberta quickly absorbed the realization that she would adorn herself with the mantle of a grieving widow and make sure that she got what was coming to her. This realistically meant that she would have to be his attendant nurse at home and that when the time came she would have to spend *all* her time with him at the hospital. This was a very tall order for Roberta, who was not used to disciplining herself in many things -- certainly not in such an emotionally charged situation like this. The other gnawing concern for Roberta was that deep down her real feeling was that she just hit the lottery and it was going to make the widow façade that much more difficult. She would have to contain her true joy.

Harry's first thoughts after the bad news had settled in were of his estate. Money was always an issue with Harry and it frequently popped up in conversations with his friends. In addition to his insurance policy, Harry had a two-family house and a baseball memorabilia card collection. He was relatively well off but he never seemed to have enough money to do the things that he wanted to do. Harry was always questioning his various golf buddies about their financial circumstances and when one was not present he would ask the others how that guy could afford to do the things he did. Harry had been a Federal employee, as had his friend Brian. He could not understand how Brian was apparently doing so well on a similar pension. He was always seeking specific numbers and Brian just laughed it off. He'd had always wondered what he was doing wrong.

Harry's awful medical diagnosis brought the money issue to the forefront in both their minds where it set up camp for the duration. Harry had heard at the hospital of a doctor in New York who performed a radical, radiation treatment which afforded some patients an extra 4 years. This doctor was not Harry's first phone call after receiving the diagnosis, Brian and his wife Catherine were. Harry wanted Brian to be a trustee of an estate that he was setting up for his children and he and Roberta went directly to Brian's house to both deliver the bad news and to make the request. Brian and Catherine later talked about the meeting and they concluded that it was surrealistic. Of course it was a shock to find out that Harry had terminal cancer. Harry acknowledged that the reality had not fully set in, but he wanted to talk about his estate and about Brian accepting the trustee responsibility. Brian agreed and he and Catherine were indirectly made privy to Harry and Roberta's wrangling over the money. Talk of the radical doctor was interspersed throughout the conversation and Harry did eventually seek his help. However, the conversation on that day was focused on the inheritance and how things were going to be divided. Harry's wish was to leave each of the three children an equal amount of money and Brian would be a co-trustee along with Roberta in overseeing and dispersing the money. Roberta would be the sole trustee for the money that was left to her daughter and this presented no problem. The unspoken reason as to why Brian had to be involved at all was, simply stated, that Harry didn't trust Roberta to follow his wishes. Problems arose when the discussion turned to dollar amounts. Roberta felt that she should be left everything in order that she might draw income from it and that when she died it would then revert to the children in some fashion. Harry wanted whatever amount they agreed upon to sit in an investment until his children were 40 years old and at that time they would receive it to perhaps help any children that they might have at that time. Another issue surfaced around the baseball collection and who would receive it. Its value (according to Harry) was between $100k-$200k, depending on how it was marketed and liquidated. Roberta wanted nothing to do with the collection. "Just give me the cash, thank you." The wrangling didn't resolve the issues that day. The tone of these negotiations was not two parents trying to figure out what was best for their children. It was that of a father who was worried about his kids getting shafted and a wife who wanted to give them **as** little as possible.

Harry did decide to seek treatment in New York with the radical doctor and this entailed going and staying in a motel on and off for several months. They stayed with relatives as well but the bills mounted up significantly. This treatment was rough going for Harry and he continued to lose weight and become frailer. However, it offered him hope and so he stuck with it. The problem with the treatment was that it not only bombarded the cancer with radiation but it also hit other vital organs. He eventually returned home disappointed in the end when it became apparent that he was not going to be one of this doctor's "miracles." At this point he sought treatment with a local oncologist but even though he tried to keep his spirits up his basic realistic, pessimism told him he was still doomed.

Money continued to be an overriding issue on a daily basis with Harry and Roberta. However, it eased some of the pressure when they insured their credit card and operated under the assumption that when Harry died Roberta would not be responsible for the debts accrued. Of course, the credit card company would have a serious problem with this if they knew that they had knowledge of Harry's prognosis. In the spirit of taking care of yourself above all else, Roberta not only had all the motel bills on the credit card but she also threw in a computer as well. This was just the tip of the iceberg of debt Roberta bragged to her friends about. Roberta's true lottery spirit surfaced when prior to Harry's death she decided it would be good for all the children to go on a cruise after Harry's death. She punched the credit card one more time and ultimately kept adding things until she amassed somewhere in the neighborhood of $20,000 worth of debt. As is often the case, in a world filled with inequities, the credit card company ultimately dismissed the debt after Harry's death and Roberta continued on with business as usual.

After his return from the radical doctor, Harry was in and out of the local hospital repeatedly and the stays varied from a few days to more than a week at a time. Roberta was having difficulty dealing with the grave inconvenience that this caused her lifestyle and particularly with the havoc it was wreaking on Cindy's senior year, sports, and graduation schedule. Cindy was a chip off the old block. Harry had been her stepfather since she was four years old and had been the only father she'd ever known. However, she never truly accepted him as "Dad". He was Harry and he was someone she had to put up with. She answered to Mom and that was that. The hospital that Harry was in and out of was located an hour away and this was a real burden for Cindy. It must have been this pressure which caused her one afternoon to blurt out that Harry had made her life miserable and now he was going to ruin her senior week. Cindy's training at the foot of Roberta shown through as she blew off several hospital visits. Roberta and Cindy had no problem whatsoever with this conduct. Cindy topped it off by accepting a free trip to Disney World with a friend while Harry lay on his impending deathbed. It worked out fine, Harry hung on until she got back and Cindy escaped suffering any guilt she might have been capable of.

Harry died peacefully at home with his family and friends at his side. Catherine had been Roberta's friend prior to and during this hardship but she was repulsed by what she witnessed in Roberta's character. Catherine had helped Roberta paint her house. She stored furniture in her garage for her even though it was a sore point with Brian. There was little appreciation for this kindness and she knew that Roberta was a user but accepted it as part of her overall personality. She had continued to be a good friend to Roberta through a lot of turmoil. However, Roberta's poor performance with Harry was too much to let pass. It must have shown because Roberta asked Catherine for an honest assessment of what was bothering her and she got it. Catherine laid it out as she saw it. She expressed her disappointment at Roberta's trying to spend as little time with a dying Harry as possible. Catherine also felt that Harry had been a good provider in the end and she felt that Roberta was unfair to his reputation by telling people that he was leaving her in a poor economic condition. When Harry was able to eat some food again towards the very end, he had requested some items and it was Catherine who had to go to the store and get them. Roberta couldn't be bothered. Catherine stifled her distaste for Cindy's conduct because she knew that Roberta would not be able to handle it. While initially Roberta accepted this criticism she ultimately rejected it and ceased speaking to Catherine and quite publicly snubbed her. Although Catherine was hurt by this conduct, it didn't come as a surprise to her. Roberta had come to Catherine's home frequently and always empty handed. She rarely returned any hospitality in her own home and she was most comfortable asking for favors. The loss of friendship with Roberta was not a loss at all. Catherine adjusted to this severing of the relationship and quickly came to realize the blessing that it was.

Ultimately, Harry's wishes were observed. His children's money was set up in the funds as he had wished. Roberta's daughter Sandra and Matthew had attended their dad well at the hospital during his last weeks and moved on with their lives knowing that they had dutifully fulfilled their responsibilities. Roberta proceeded to wear her widow's mantel most comfortably but slipped up somewhat when her perky giddiness shown through. Some people wrote it off as a reaction to stress rather than a breakdown in her façade – which it was.

It was nine or ten months later that a memorial service for Harry was held on the beach near his home. He'd been cremated and his ashes were spread over the ocean he always enjoyed. Attendees were asked to speak a few words if they cared to and of course some did. Roberta was a well-practiced widow at this point and there were no chinks in her armor this day.

The stand out of the ceremony was Cindy and the tearful performance she was able to manufacture for the occasion. She could barely choke her way through all the loving words she had written for the man who had almost ruined her senior week. Ones actions will always echo much louder and meaningful than any words. It's often said that our departed loved ones look over us from above. I like to picture ole Harry as preoccupied these days.

Did I tell you this one?

## Silly Me

I was at the Publix supermarket down the street from where I live in Vero Beach, Florida. I had my shopping in the cart as I walked out of the market and looked for my car at the usual area where I parked. Not there. I looked around at the second area where I would park if it was crowded. Not there. It wasn't anywhere. I checked out the entire lot and my beloved Buick Enclave was gone. Oh shit. This is a problem. I had my gun on the console. That is a real problem. So, I decided to call 911 and get the information out as quickly as possible. I called and a very pleasant woman took my information and said that they would send a unit over shortly. I ended the call and as I looked at my phone I realized that I had my wife's car keys in my hand. I felt like a moron. We brought Linda's Honda Accord to Florida this year from North Carolina, our primary home. I immediately looked up and there was her car sitting right where I normally parked.

I was very relieved and realized I had to call 911 right away and call off the police. I called back and got the same pleasant woman on the phone. I explained what had happened with the different cars and apologized profusely for my dumb mistake. I kiddingly said that I had a senior moment. She laughed and consoled me by saying; "Senior moments are a way of life around here, it happens all the time. After all, this is Florida.

# Jimmy Tee

When you work in law enforcement, you are constantly surrounded by filthy language, it comes with the territory. The banter is foul and politically incorrect, but it's an integral part of the story. More importantly, it's an accurate depiction of true events which occurred during the mid-1970's in New York Office of the FBI. In the best tradition of Joe Friday, some names have been changed in part to protect the innocent.

"Jimmy Tee" was born James Anthony Targiano in Bensonhurst, Brooklyn in 1940. He lived in that area until he was in his mid-twenties when he got married and moved to Queens. Jimmy got the nickname "Jimmy Tee" partially because his last name began with the letter T. However, it was primarily because of his penchant for wearing Fruit of the Loom string Tee shirts -- affectionately referred to as; "Guinea Tees." Jimmy had a good build and in the warm weather he liked to show off his biceps and an assortment of tattoos that he had acquired during a wayward youth.

Jimmy hadn't married Angela Fererese because he had knocked her up, but because Angela's father Luke told him that if he didn't do the right thing, he would personally see to it that Jimmy went through life trying to recover from ten broken fingers. "I'll break your fucking hands and stick them up your ass" was the exact quote.

Luke was rumored to have been half mobbed-up and killed another longshore man in a dispute over a lousy $1200 debt. It was clear to all who knew him that you didn't screw with Luke. Jimmy moved to Queens mainly to distance himself from Luke and also to show his probation officer that he was getting a new start in life. Jimmy had gotten arrested for his involvement in a stolen car ring and had the bad fortune of having had an acetylene cutting torch in his hands when the cops hit the chop shop that he was working at. Jimmy did eighteen months at Riker's Island Prison where he aligned himself with the mobbed up Italian prisoners thus protecting himself from the Black Gangs that fed on unaligned inmates. Jimmy hated Blacks and he was quite comfortable with this arrangement.

When Jimmy moved to Queens he took over a luncheonette on Hillside Ave. in the Jamaica Estates area and this paid the bills. He always had some young kid running the luncheonette and the only one he had to pay a decent salary was the cook. This arrangement freed up Jimmy to pursue his real career as a shylock. Shylock, of course, was the relentless money lender in Shakespeare's "Merchant of Venice" and Jimmy was just that, a relentless money lender. He put money on the streets and collected interest, known as the vigorous or "Vig", at usurious rates on a weekly basis. Now in New York you can't just set up shop and lend money not only because it's illegal but because in the 1970's, at least, you had to pay tribute to the local mob "Capo" for the privilege. If it were found out that you were working the streets without permission nothing good was going to happen to you.

Jimmy, it turned out, was pretty successful with his loan business and it became apparent that he had the local Capo's blessing.

Jimmy came to my attention when I was working on an FBI Organized Crime squad that was operating out of a satellite office in Levittown, Long Island. This office had a dozen agents with a designated Agent in Charge which was a very thankless job. You were in charge of people who were really your equal because there was no official promotion attached to this Agent in Charge position. The unfortunate senior agent who took this assignment was a highly respected agent named Joe Fanning. The project turned out to be very successful for a number of reasons and the primary one was the popularity of Joe. Although he wasn't that much older than most of us, Joe was a bit of a father figure and he was a talented investigator who was a great family man. No one wanted to be the one who screwed it up for Joe. The other main reason for its success was the fact that you came and went as you pleased and with this group there were enough self-starters to keep the other guys busy. Jimmy Abbott was the most aggressive of the group and also probably the best liked guy. When he asked for help with a project no one refused.

The office was physically located on the second floor of a two story, freestanding office building in Levittown, Long Island and the space was nothing more than a large open room with a dozen or so desks that had the look and feel of a police precinct on the lower East side of Manhattan. Someone always had a cigarette or cigar going, and since there were no women assigned to the unit, the language was usually locker room at best. (I told you this story was politically incorrect). It was no secret to the other tenants of the building that the FBI occupied this office but the office was not open to the public. We took no complaints from walk- ins and our phone lines were private. Every morning guys would arrive with their coffee and bagels and more often than not it turned in to a bull session with jokes being told and guys "ranking" on one another. I remember the guy from a credit agency down the hall knocking on the door one morning and asking us to keep it down, we were disturbing his employees. Joe Fanning in a rare moment of ire asked us to cool it and left the office a little perturbed. Joe was out the door about a minute before Bernie Welsh started to refer to him as "Joey the Prick", a name that stuck for years much to Bernies' shame.

John Egan was an old time ITSP (Interstate Transportation of Stolen Property) truck theft agent who was a nuts and bolts guy and who was as much cop as investigator. He had put in his time and no one expected him to generate a whole lot of original work but he was always available if needed. No one had a problem with this but we used to laugh at the pile of files that he kept in a work box on his desk. We all knew that these were props and whenever John wasn't around the topic always came up. One afternoon an order of KFC chicken was ordered in for lunch and the usual bull session went into gear during the lunch. Egan's work box came up for discussion and Kenny Giel had the thought that perhaps a barometer of activity regarding these files could be established. He placed two whistles clean chicken leg bones into the middle of the pile of files and the calendar watch ensued. Now you must understand that in those days all files, every thirty days, had to reflect in writing an update of investigative activity or an explanation as to why no new investigation had occurred. It was almost five months to the day, the morning that John, while searching through his work box for god knows what exclaimed, while gingerly picking up two very dry skinny chicken bones , "What the fuck are these doing here?". The room erupted, Egan didn't have a clue as to what the laughter was about, the guy from the Credit agency was at the door again and Joe Fanning left the office, his head shaking with the a look of resignation only arrived at by a manager who knows that he has lost control.

Jimmy Abbott arrived at the office one morning and asked me if I would sit in on an interview that afternoon that he had scheduled with a citizen named Herb Marcus who had called the New York Office to complain about being threatened by a "business associate". Jimmy usually worked with Kenny Giel and I inquired as to Kenny's whereabouts. He responded that Kenny had taken a day off to wall paper a study room in is house because his wife was complaining arduously that he had precious little time for her or the house since he started working in this new project that was thirty miles closer to the house. As it turned out, Kenny did a great job of installing the paper, which had a pattern of flying ducks. Unfortunately, the ducks were gracefully loping along on their backs. That's right, they were installed upside down and that pretty much explains the way that marriage went, graceful loping along on its back. However, that's another story for Kenny to tell. Jimmy had Marcus were coming in after lunch, so I filled the morning with paper work and phone calls and tried to catch up on a bit of a backlog that had amassed.

During lunch, the usual rap of conversation was going on with a couple of guys talking about sports and making plans to stop for a couple of "pops" after work. Bobby Levy, one of the self-starters, was at lunch and this in itself was unusual because he virtually worked out of his house. This was an unofficial privilege that was granted to guys who produced and indeed, Bobby was a producer. I remember that he told the story of a first office agent of the 1950's whose name was Hal Landreth and who I coincidentally came to know at the end of my career in North Carolina. It seems that Landreth was assigned to a mid-western office of the FBI and that any time he needed an automobile, being a rookie, he could only get the keys for an old Hudson Hornet that everyone in the office shunned. As fate would have it this Hudson Hornet was green and Landreth, possessing a fine sense of humor, took to signing in and out on the air as the "Green Hornet".

Apparently one afternoon, Hal reported on the air with his usual "The Green Hornet is 10-8 at 2:30 pm" with the misfortune of having the Special Agent in Charge, Howard Doolittle standing next to the radio operator. The pompous Doolittle, who was appropriately sir named, demanded that the radio operator tell him which agent was referring to himself as the Green Hornet on the air.. The radio operator wasn't about to hand up a nice guy like Hal and claimed not to recognize the voice. Mr. Bureau drone Doolittle took control of the microphone and in a most authoritative and supercilious manner demanded that the Green Hornet identify himself at once on the air by his proper signal number. There was a long pause and a voice piped up " He may be green but he ain't *that* green." Doolittle never put the name and the car together and was forever marked as the boob that he was.

Marcus arrived on time for the interview and that in itself was contradictory from what our experiences had been with shylock victims. That was the only thing, however that strayed from what we had come to expect from these kind of guys. Marcus was about 40 years old, balding, overweight and unkempt. His clothes were dirty but not as dirty as the old dinged up Chevy Caprice that he had arrived in. He needed a shave and a shower would have helped. His story was a familiar song to our ears. It began with the fact that he owned a bagel shop in Glen Cove, Long Island that, according to him, was doing poorly and in order to keep it afloat he had turned to Jimmy Tee for some street money. In reality the shop was doing quite well and Marcus' money problems arose from his voracious sports betting appetite. He was another loser and it didn't take much prying to get the truth out of him. The bookie had leaned on him big time to square his account and he had learned of Jimmy Tee from another gambler buddy of his. Jimmy lent him $15,000 which solved his problem short term and had he stopped gambling he could have survived the outlandish payments to Jimmy. He didn't and Jimmy was all over him to pay back his money.

Marcus related that Jimmy was threatening him with physical harm and that Jimmy had come to the store one evening, cleaned out the register and slapped him around.

Jimmy Abbott ran some background checks on both Jimmy Tee and the bookie and both had records that lent credibility to Marcus' story. The next step that we pursued in this investigation was to get Jimmy Tee on tape. We had to record him on the telephone with Marcus verifying some of the facts of the allegation. If things went along and we successfully indicted Jimmy Tee we would then try and squeeze him for co-operation and get not only the bookie but also the Capo that Jimmy was inevitably working for. Marcus had left it with Jimmy that he would meet him one night the following week and that he would pay Jimmy $2,000 towards the debt.

The initial telephone call was a big deal for a number of reasons. First we had to get Herb Marcus to overcome his extreme nervousness about doing it and to do it in such a fashion that we allowed Jimmy plenty of rope to hang himself. Secondly, the purpose of the call was not only to confirm a meeting between the two but also to have Jimmy arrive at it in such a fashion that he would make it clear that he was there to get his money and by force if necessary. With these goals in mind, we bought Herb lunch, soothed his frayed nerves and convinced him that the only way he was going to get out of this mess was to do what we told him. He agreed and it was determined that the best time to call Jimmy was at 6:00pm in the evening and that is just what we did.

The recorder had been tested and fresh batteries were installed. I didn't like to use the electric chord when we were making these calls, if possible, because I was afraid of the electric going out for some reason and the evidence would then be lost. We had put a preamble on the tape which identified the agent who was conducting the monitoring as well as the time, location and the participants in the call. We were ready to go and much to my surprise so was Herb Marcus. Jimmy Abbott had done a masterful job of pumping him up and by the time he got done with him, Marcus was ready to take on the world. Herb dialed Jimmy's number and his wife answered the phone. She asked who it was, Herb identified himself and Jimmy shortly appeared on the phone. Herb got right to it and told Jimmy that he wasn't going to meet him next week that he was having trouble raising the money and that Jimmy would just have to wait. Boom, it was the Fourth of July. Jimmy bit hook, line, sinker and was about to take out a piece of the boat as well. "Angela, get out of the room and close the door." There was a noticeable door slam in the background and Jimmy got right into it.

"Listen to me you Jew fuck, who do you think you're talking to. You'll be there Tuesday and you'll have my money or I'll take this phone and shove it up your ass. If you ain't there, they'll be looking for your fat fucking body in the Long Island sound". A death threat, just as Herb had predicted, and a piece of good evidence. Herb tried to stammer a response but Jimmy obligingly continued "Shut the fuck up! If you're not there I'm gonna find you and make you suck a thousand n*##@r dicks. You understand me! A thousand n*@#&r dicks!" Jimmy was truly worked up but as you can see this did not hamper his racist creativity. Jimmy was screaming into the phone; "I don't care if you have to pimp out that flabby bitch you married or if you got to sell one of your kids, be there with my fucking money or your dead. Do you hear me asshole?" Herb said yes and we gave him the high sign to agree with Jimmy and he told Jimmy he was sorry and that he would do his best to get the money. Jimmy was only mollified a little and he continued, " Be there or your finished." and with this the phone went dead. Herb was nervous again and we were jubilant. He had acknowledged the debt and had made a threat over the phone. Things were going along according to plan and the meeting could lead to Jimmy Tee's arrest and the beginning of the wrap up of the investigation.

The big night came and we went about preparing Herb Marcus for the meeting that he was going to have with Jimmy Tee. The meeting had to be recorded. Videotaping was just coming into regular use in the Bureau at this time but because the meeting was taking place at night and because of the poor lighting in the bagel shop parking lot, this was ruled out. The best method of the time was to use a Nagra body recorder. A Nagra is a high quality Swiss machine that was about the size of a small, thin paperback novel. Sometimes this could be secreted in an article of clothing or strapped to a person's leg. The problem of course is that it wouldn't survive a thorough pat down and Herb knew this. He was already to nervous for our liking so we opted to skip the Nagra and to use a small transmitter. The transmitter was hidden in a pair of cowboy boots and this worked fine for Marcus and helped to ease his nervousness. We often used these transmitters in conjunction with the Nagra because they provided live coverage of the event and allowed you to make better informed decisions as things were occurring. Their drawback was there unreliability. They were often static ridden and intermittent with their transmissions but because we would be able to get a van virtually on top of them for the meeting, we decided to go with it. The van would record the transmitters output and provide us with visual surveillance of the meeting.

Jimmy Tee was late for the meeting. Everyone was getting nervous. Herb was inside his shop knowing that we were monitoring him passing comments on the transmitter about wanting to close the business and wrap it up for the night. We had set up surveillance at Jimmy Tee's house but he had never showed. If he was coming to the meeting, he was coming from somewhere else. The bagel shop was normally closed at 9:30 pm and it was fast approaching that time now. We sent an agent inside to tell Herb that he should wait until 10:00 pm to close the shop and he was not happy to hear this.  The different guys were conjecturing over their car radios as to what might be making Jimmy Tee late for the meeting.  Ken Giel asked anxiously on the air to no one in particular, "I wonder what's keeping him?"  There was a brief silence and a voice responded  "Maybe he's out rounding up a thousand n*&&#r's."  There was a moment of deafening silence followed by a strong eruption of laughter. I have a strong suspicion as to who passed the comment but no one ever has or will own up to it.

Jimmy Tee rolled in just before 10 and waived at Herb to come outside. The plan was for Herb to beg for more time and to give Jimmy only $500 and to set up a meeting for the following week.  This would allow us to identify more victims of Jimmy through surveillance's but of course he was not going to be a happy camper with Herb Marcus.   We told Herb that if things got out of hand we would intercede and arrest Jimmy on the spot but we didn't mention to Herb that it's a judgement call as to what getting out of hand means.  Herb rushed out to greet him and as planned, steered Jimmy to the alleyway alongside of the store.  This gave us both clear transmissions for the transmitter and a perfect eyeball for the guys in the van.  The transmitter was on an FBI universal channel that we had cleared for the evening and this allowed everybody who was in range to listen to the conversation on their car radios.  All the units had hand held radios as well for the purpose of communicating with each other.

Jimmy Tee got right to it. "Where's the money?"  Herb responded "Jimmy I could only come up with $500.  My wife has got some money coming from her sister but I won't have it until next week." "You fat fuck" and with that Jimmy hit Herb in the right eye with what amounted to a half jab, half punch shot. Herb hit deck better than Sonny Liston had for Mohammed Ali's phantom punch.  Jimmy was standing over him, "You piece of shit.  When I lent you the money everything was 'Jimmy don't
96

worry I can pay you back on time'. I oughta take my belt off and beat you silly". Everyone's adrenaline was pumping and we were waiting for the signal to move in for the arrest but Jim Abbott had us hold up. It appeared that Jimmy Tee didn't have a gun and as long as Herb was on the ground it didn't look like Jimmy was going to do much of anything else. Herb was excitedly trying to let us know that he was in peril. "Jimmy why did you hit me in the eye? Everything is blurry. I can't see." Jimmy Tee then grabbed his crotch and said "See this? I'm coming next week and if you don't have the rest of the money I'm gonna stick it up your ass." I had an eyeball on the action and both Kenny Giel and I saw him grab his crotch. We couldn't help ourselves as we started laughing. The pressure was off. Jimmy Tee was talking about coming back next week so he had adjusted to the $500 payment. Abbott was content to let Herb take a little beating for good evidentiary reasons and if we didn't have to arrest him that night we bought the bonus week of surveillance's to identify other victims. Jimmy Tee must have been getting concerned about passersby activity because he reached down and started helping Herb get up. "Jimmy don't hit me again. I swear I can get the money by next week." Herb was begging. "Shut up you stupid shit. You're gonna have that money next week or you're a fucking dead man." Herb started thanking Jimmy Tee profusely and Jimmy told him to go in the store and bring out a dozen of bagels. "Make sure I get the thirteenth free one." He wanted his free thirteenth baker's dozen bagel. Giel and I were howling. This guy goes from "I'm gonna kill you." to "Don't forget my free bagel" in one sentence.

Herb came out with the bagels and after a couple of more threats, Jimmy Tee drove away from the scene. We took Herb back to our office to debrief him, take photographs and collect our equipment. Herb understandably was very upset that we hadn't arrested Jimmy on the spot but Abbott soothed him and by the time we got him to the hospital, Herb thought he was John Wayne again.

We had a successful week following Jimmy Tee around. We identified what we believed to be several more of Jimmy's victims and determined with the United States Attorney's Office that we would arrest Jimmy at the next meeting with Herb Marcus. This happened as we planned and Jimmy Tee was arrested at the meeting with Herb Marcus. He had marked money on him that we had given to Marcus and we collected some more threats on tape and photographs of the entire transaction. Basically, Jimmy Tee was screwed. He was arraigned and set free on a 10% OR bond. (Own-recognizance)

After a couple of weeks, Jimmy Abbott and I decided it was time to go and have a talk with Jimmy Tee and see if he was interested in helping us out. He had a couple of weeks to sit and stew and we surmised that we might just have been able to present him with an escape hatch that he would be willing to take. Now Jimmy Tee of course was represented by an attorney but in those days it was a grey area as to whether or not you could approach a defendant without his attorney. It wasn't a grey area to us.

Abbott and I sat around the corner on a side street from Jimmy's Hillside Ave. luncheonette. Jimmy's car was parked a couple of cars in front of us and when he came out of the luncheonette and approached the car, we walked up and surprised him. "Hey Jimmy, remember me?" Abbott began the conversation. He must of been kidding, I remember musing to myself. Was it likely that Jimmy Tee was going to forget a 375lb. cop who had arrested him less than a month ago? "Yeah, of course", Jimmy nervously replied. "Relax, we're here just to talk to you. You don't have to say anything. We want you to sit in our car and listen to what we have to say. When we're done, you can ask questions or just get up and leave. You have my word no strings attached." Abbott could be very persuasive in a short period of time. I chimed in "Jimmy we're in a position to try and help you out. All you have to do is listen. We want to give you something to think about. When were done, like my partner says, you can talk or walk, whatever you want to do". "You're not jerking me off?" Jimmy asked warily. "You have my word" Abbott responded. "Let's sit in the car. I'll drive a couple of blocks away from the store and the whole thing won't take a half hour". And that is what we did.

I didn't waste any time and got right to the heart of our presentation. Abbott and I of course had worked out our pitch and I made much ado about setting up a cassette player that I had with me. I put a cassette into the machine and asked Jimmy Tee to pay attention to it and see if he recognized anyone. The player was a little tinny and it took Jimmy a few minutes to realize that the tape that was playing was his voice. He started to look a little uncomfortable and then the tape barked out "Shut the fuck up! If you're not there, I'm gonna find you and make you suck a thousand ni**r dicks." I turned the player off. Abbott told Jimmy that this presented a real problem for Jimmy. He explained that this tape was evidence that would be used at his trial and that needless to say, this remark was offensive not only to any black juror that might be on his jury but probably to all the white jurors as well. Jimmy Tee was truly taken aback. He didn't say anything. He didn't have to, it was in his face. Abbott continued that this was only part of the problem. The other part consisted of the make-up of the judges in the Eastern District of New York, the Federal district where Jimmy Tee's trial would take place. Abbott pointed out that there were approximately eight judges in the district at any one time and that Judge Bramley who was Black was a permanent judge in the district. Abbott was warming up to his subject real well and he continued that Jimmy Tee probably didn't know this but the way they picked cases was literally through a lottery. This was done in order to insure fairness in the assignments.  He pointed out to Jimmy that he had what amounted to a one in eight chance of drawing a black judge who was going to hear this tape and who would ultimately be responsible for his sentencing if he were convicted.  I was watching Jimmy closely and he looked frightened.  He hadn't looked nervous when we arrested him but he was flushed now and when we asked him how he felt, he just grunted. We finished the pitch between us by telling him that we would talk to the United States Attorney about the possibility of a plea based upon his cooperation.  We made it clear that ultimately we wanted him to cooperate with us against whoever he was working for.  He listened and when given the opportunity to ask us questions, he surprised us by getting out of the car and standing on the sidewalk.  He spoke hardly a word.  He just said that he would think about it and walked back to the luncheonette.  I never spoke to Jimmy Tee again.

The investigation went into Limbo for a couple of weeks while we waited for the case to move through the court system.  Abbott and I turned our attention to other matters and weren't giving the case much thought until we received a call one morning from the United States Attorney's office.  The prosecutor informed us that Jimmy Targiano had drawn Judge Bramley for his case and that his attorney had called and indicated that Jimmy wanted to come in and plead guilty to the charges.  There would be no plea bargaining. He was coming in and pleading straight up and throwing himself on the mercy of the court.  The tape recording would not be entered into evidence and the judge would not know that it existed.  In the end, Jimmy was sentenced to seven years in prison.

Herb Marcus sold his bagel shop and moved to Florida to start over.  I don't know if this meant a new bagel business or a career at the dog tracks, probably both.  The Levittown "Module" as it had become known, although uniquely successful, was disbanded for manpower needs and the agents were assigned to different offices on Long Island and Manhattan.. I personally moved onto multiple endeavors after retirement, but nothing matched the people and great times with the FBI.

# Art Donovan

My stories are replete with assorted Bronx tales revolving around family and life events. I'm breaking the mold and would like to tell you about an encounter that I had with a famous non-family, Bronx boy; Art Donovan. Sometime in the late eighties or early nineties, I was returning from Ft. Mead where I had been on business with a group of my fellow FBI Agents. We made a detour to a country club on the outskirts of Baltimore that was owned by Art Donovan. Art was a Hall of Fame football lineman with the Baltimore Colts during the 1950s. Several of my friends were associated with the FBI Marine Corps Association and they had an award that they were presenting to Art who had been a private in the Marine Corps during WWII and who had fought in the battles of Luzon and Iwo Jima. I looked that up, Art Donovan wasn't the kind of guy to toot his own horn, he didn't tell me. On the contrary, he was the king of self-deprecating humor. Check out his appearances on the David Letterman Show on YouTube, they're a scream.

We arrived at the club at 11:00 am and they installed us in the bar while they went looking for Art. He came in shortly thereafter and he filled all the space behind the bar. This guy was massive. His playing weight was 275 lbs. but he had to be 350 lbs. when I saw him. I shook his hand and it swallowed my hand up. He was just a big boy. He offered the lads a beer and they accepted and he served them some Schaefer beer. Schaefer beer had been a New York staple years before but as far as Art was concerned it was a current delicacy. After they conducted their business with them, I mentioned to Art that I was from the Bronx. He perked up and told me that he went to Mount St. Michael's and that he grew up in St Phillip Neri parish, which was located on the Concourse. He said that he got a scholarship to Notre Dame for football but that he had a problem with the famous coach, Frank Leahy. It seems Frank thought that drinking and partying weren't helpful for your football career. Art said that things weren't working out, so he joined the Marines.

I told him I grew up just down the Concourse in St. Simon Stock parish and that I had played sandlot football at Harris Field in his neighborhood. He got a big smile on his face and asked me if the guy who had fingers missing on his hand still sold hotdogs when I played there. I said he did and he laughed saying they always wondered if they were floating around somewhere in the cart. I told him great minds think alike. We all thought the same thing too.

I asked him if he had been back to New York recently and he said he hadn't but that the hotdog talk reminded him of his last visit from years earlier. He was with an old buddy of his and he described him as a guy who could give him a run for his money when it came to eating. They were down by the World Trade Center and they got a hold of a hotdog vendor and told him to get ready, they were really hungry. He said that they ate to capacity, washing it down with a bunch of Pepsi. He said we were with the guy for a couple of hours. When he got done he asked the guy, "What do I owe you?" The guy told him $10. He looked at me with a wink and said; "Hotdogs were a quarter back then." I imagine these guys ate 40 hot dogs, and they weren't stuffing them down like the "Nathans Famous" Coney Island contestants -- these guys were truly enjoying them. I believed him then and I still do now. I savor my contact with the great Art Donovan, a Bronx boy in every sense of the word. The world is short of true characters like Art Donovan and for certain the NFL of today doesn't hold a candle to the simpler greatness of the footballers of Art Donovan's era.

# Hola

After I retired from the FBI I did compliance anti-money laundering contract work. This amounted to working at different banks around the country for three months at a time. Different banks failed Federal audits for poorly monitoring money laundering activity in their accounts. As a remedy, they would have to hire my friend's company of ex-federal investigators to come in and review accounts and usually pay a hefty fine.

I was working in a bank in Miami on the famed Brickell Ave whose customers were almost exclusively South Americans and whose employees were mainly Cuban Americans. It was really an enlightening experience. The first thing that jumped out at me was the fact that the woman came to work dressed up every day. I'm talking high-heel dressed up. I worked at several banks, and the back room women employees were always very casually dressed. These Miami women were a standout. I was in an office area with about a dozen other guys like myself and it wasn't unusual to have someone come in and say "Did anybody see that girl with the red dress this morning?" I knew exactly what they were talking about because there was a "red dress" girl floating around the building every day.

My story isn't about the red-dress girls but rather about a group of ladies in the office who were closer to my age and who I walked by every morning. These ladies were friendly and the first time one of them smiled and said "Hola", I was surprised. It became the routine where I would walk by in the morning and say "Hola" and wave to everybody. I got a kick out of it. Look at me, I'm speaking Spanish.

At this time I was in my early 60s with grey hair and a full closely white-trimmed beard. As I walked by one morning, one of the ladies waved me over to her desk. I had never really spoken to the ladies and didn't know what to expect. She smiled and told me that she and her friends thought I looked like Kenny Rogers. Naturally, I was flattered and told them so.

The next morning on an impulse, I bought a dozen Dunkin Donuts and brought them into work with me. I went over and placed the donuts on the desk of the lady who had called me over. All the ladies were looking at me as I leaned over her desk and sang "You picked a fine time to leave me, Lucille". Everybody laughed including me because it was funny. I waved "Hola" and sauntered off to my desk feeling pretty cool.

I knew that every day around 3pm a group of Latino employees gathered together in the break room and made Cuban expresso coffee. They put it in little paper cups and sipped on it like it was whiskey. It was a great idea at that time of the day because I was always falling asleep. To my surprise that afternoon, my friendly lady friend walked into our office area with a donut and a Cuban coffee and put it on my desk, "Hola". My buddies were very impressed as was I and I enjoyed the notoriety.

By the way, the Cuban expresso is like a 5-hour-energy drink. It really gave me a lift. The ladies let me know that I was welcome to come in any day and have a Cuban coffee.  I often went in and got one to go and never got tired of our new friendships.

# Momma Hood

After graduating high school, I moved on to Manhattan College. That fact that Manhattan College was actually located in the Bronx should have made me suspicious of the whole experience. During the summers I worked at the Breezy Point Surf Club as a cabana boy and bartender. This was a great job. I literally made enough money from tips to pay my entire college tuition without taking any loans. Years later when I bragged about this at a family party, my "over-served" Mother chimed in. She revealed that not only had I paid my tuition but also half of my brother Pat's. What?! This was news to me. Please elaborate Mom, tell me more. My mother laughed.

The story goes that every Sunday night I would come home from my jobs at the Surf Club with pockets literally stuffed with money. It wasn't unusual to make four or five hundred dollars a week and I would leave the money on top of the dresser and go to bed exhausted. Mom and I had an understanding. She would deposit the money in the bank for my school bills and leave me with fifteen or twenty dollars for the week to come. I never kept track. After all, this was my mother who was taking care of things. Well, as Mom confessed, Pat and I both went to Manhattan and our bills came due at the same time. Pat worked as a Parkie at Rockaway Beach during the summer making $67 a week sleeping under the boardwalk. What I didn't know was that Pat was dependent on my parents and student loans to pay his tuition. Mom didn't always have the money to supplement Pat's bills so, you got it, she would dip into that other pot of money -- my money. Of course, I never knew anything. I didn't even know what my bank balance was, much less that Mom was borrowing from it. All I knew was that my bills always got paid and I had pocket money from my job as a school bus driver with the Riverdale Country Day School. (A little distraction here, this school's most famous graduate was JFK.) I never got mad about this. Honestly, I laughed when I found out about it and spent the next twenty years telling Pat it was OK and there was no need to thank me. Pat always said that I didn't have to worry about getting either the "thank you" or the money. I'm smiling now as I write this. I would kid my mother over the years and when she was visiting at my house I'd say, "Sit tight Mom I'll be right back, I'm going upstairs to count my money" We always had a good laugh over it.

Mom was the queen of making things work. There were seven of us in a two-bedroom, five-story walk-up. Dad had two jobs and Mom was the glue that made it all go. I loved her and Pat dearly and this is just one example of her inventiveness that helped us all get a good start in our lives. She was a special woman -- job well done Mom.

## Jackie Mason

Jackie Mason was the personification of the Jewish Comedian. While he was born in Sheboygan, Wisconsin, he grew up on New York's Lower East Side in an orthodox Jewish family. He was an ordained Rabbi and he was simply hilarious. He perfected his trade on the famous Borscht Belt of the Catskill Mountains in New York. It consisted of a series of hotels that were famous for their Jewish comedians. Jackie had a heavy Jewish accent which I find charming and political correctness is not his strong point.

I had an Aunt whose name was May Mason. She was my father's sister and her children were my first cousins, Danny and Francis Mason. Sadly, they have both passed away. However, they were both good, honorable men with wonderful families that I simply don't see often enough. I guess this begs the question, were they Jewish? A little research determined that Mason is a Scotch, English name with a branch in Ireland. It turns out that Jackie was born Jacob Moshe Maza and Mason was a stage name. Wouldn't it have been fun if you found out that Jackie Mason was a distant cousin? No luck there but we proudly claim Sean Hannity of Conservative Television and Radio fame, as a cousin on my father's side. My father's brother Connie

Flynn had a daughter, Lilian, my first cousin who was Sean's mother. Again, some noble and decent people that I don't see enough.

Jackie Mason was famous for his one-man shows and it was sometime in the mid-1990s that he had one of these on Broadway. Someone had given me a video copy of this show and it was devastatingly funny. Jackie skewered all races and creeds. He was relentless on the Irish, Italians, Jews, Blacks, Women, Hispanics, I mean everybody. Here are a couple of examples of Jackie's one-liner witticisms.

"My father was a very successful businessman but he was ruined during the depression. A stockbroker jumped out of a window and landed on his pushcart."

"I have enough money to last the rest of my life unless I buy something."

"Ladies and Gentlemen you can't please everyone. Take my girlfriend, I think she's the most remarkable woman in the world but that's me. My wife on the other hand doesn't see it that way."

And finally, "It's no longer a question of staying healthy; it's a question of finding a disease you like."

I like these wisecracking kind of quotes, I always have. His show was loaded with them.

I had recently viewed Jackie's video so it was fresh in my mind as I walked down Lexington Ave. in Manhattan with my FBI partner, Ted Savadel. Our work frequently took us to the Upper East Side of New York and we loved the neighborhood. It was a sunny day with a lot of people on the streets. Of course, who do I spot ahead walking towards me with his red dyed hair and a tall blond woman on his arm, none other than the one and only, Jackie Mason. As he approached, I shouted to him, "Jackie, I saw your show, it was great." He smiled as we passed and I was glowing in the fun of having spotted Jackie Mason. After I passed him, I heard a loud shout "Hey, hey." I turned around and it was Jackie saying to me "Really?" I said "Really." We stopped, he laughed, turned to the pretty lady, and said "See, I told you." I laughed and we all walked on. That was over forty years ago and I'm still chuckling. I love Jackie Mason

# St. Patrick's Day Parade

If you're an Irish American in New York you have some kind of a connection to the St. Patrick's Day Parade. My earliest memories of the parade were house parties on parade day where corn beef and cabbage were featured. Mom, Dad, Uncle Tommy, Aunt Maime, Uncle Eddy, and Aunt Betty were the Irish stronghold celebrating our heritage. All my cousins were involved at different times. We played Ruby Murray's album; "When Irish eyes are smiling." Everybody watched the parade on WPIX TV waiting for County Waterford to pass by to see if we would recognize relatives. You knew who was marching and the Fennesseys in particular were always well represented. We always marveled how American-born broadcaster Jack McCarthy developed a brogue for the day.

I remember vaguely going to the parade with someone when I was very young but I remember much more vividly when I marched. You see when I was twelve years old I was a member of the St Simon Stock Sea Cadets. I proudly wore my navy uniform with its white gob hat and white leggings. I remember pestering my mother until she took me on the subway to somewhere in Manhattan to purchase the uniform. I had no idea what a hardship it must have been for her but I wanted what I wanted and that's that. I felt so important. I went to meetings every week where Commander O'Shea and his wife were in charge. Mr. Mangum was the music director and he taught me how to play the drums. I played them all, the snare, tenor, and bass drums. They taught us how to march and it was a full-time job keeping us in line and well-behaved.

I marched in the parade twice when it was at the largesse of one of the counties that followed the "give the kids a chance" dictum. We were irrefutably terrible and I'm truly grateful they gave us the opportunity and didn't even laugh at us. I loved it. We marched in several other parades but this one was the big leagues. I played the bass because I was bigger than the other kids and able to carry it the distance. Besides the drums, the other main instrument in the band was the glockenspiel. The glockenspiel was played by the girls. Our big number was "The Wearing of the Green". Commander O'Sheas red-headed daughter was the lead girl. The boys ogled her from afar but she was unapproachable since she was considered an "older woman" at thirteen.

Later in life as an adult I would go to the parade with Linda and view it from the Central Park side of Fifth Ave. across the street from the Guggenheim Museum. We would meet up with all our FBI friends and laugh and cheer at the unbelievable amount of people that we knew who were marching. When I was an officer in the FBI Emerald Society we would throw a party in the Seventh Regiment Armory on Park Ave. I remember Maryellen, Margaret, and a contingent of family showing up one time and there was no room in the inn. The place was a zoo. The parade had gotten a bad reputation at one time for drunken behavior. Mayor Ed Koch cleaned the parade up by getting the Catholic High Schools to stop giving the day off and by making copious arrests.

To this day, no matter where I am, I still celebrate St. Patrick's Day by watching; "The Quiet Man" with John Wayne and Maureen O'Hara. If I can get my hands on some blood pudding I also make us an Irish breakfast. I love St Patrick's Day With all its' fond memories and I hope this story has triggered some of yours.

# Jimmy Blessington

Jimmy Blessington was my very good friend Mary Abbott's brother. He was a laid-back kind of guy who was an ironworker. He was a very good family man who was liked by all. While he was a man of few words, when he spoke he was always worth listening to. Unfortunately, Jimmy was diagnosed with late-stage cancer and wound up in the hospital knowing that he was nearing the end of his life.

John Blessington was Jimmy's brother and a different kind of guy than Jimmy. John was a gentleman as well who was a school teacher who lived in Manhattan. John was a sophisticated man who enjoyed the museums and theaters of the city. The brothers were quite different but equally respectable men. John was very distraught over Jimmy's illness.

When John went to visit Jimmy in the hospital, he found it very hard to keep his composure. He tried talking to Jimmy about his condition but kept breaking down. Jimmy felt bad that his brother was having such a bad time and consoled him with the following words. "John, it's not that bad. After all, it's not like they told me I'm going to die and you're not."

Like I said, Jimmy was a man of few words but when he spoke he was worth listening to.

## The Jackie Gleason Show

Now that my generation has taken a seat at the old people's table at weddings one of the things we can brag about was that we were there when TV came to the common man. My cousin Margaret suggested that I should talk about old TV shows and their influence in one of my stories. After all, as kids in the Bronx, we remember when our families got their first televisions. While TV was invented in the 1920s, it really hit the mass market in the late 40s and early 50s. I know in my house there were two immediate 'must-watch' shows that were there right from the start; "The Jackie Gleason Show" and Bishop Fulton J Sheen's "Life is Worth Living". I knew Bishop Sheen was very dramatic and used a blackboard like my teachers but I never really understood what he was talking about. On the other hand, everybody knew what Gleason was talking about.

If there was ever a "larger-than-life" guy, it was Jackie Gleason. Born in Bushwick, Brooklyn in a tenement, his father walked out on the family during the depression when Jackie was nine years old. Gleason's mother worked as a subway token booth attendant to support them. However, she passed away when he was just 19 years old. By that time, Jackie was already scrambling to make a living as a comedian in different clubs and formats in New York and the surrounding area. Gleason's rise to fame included work in virtually *all* aspects of entertainment that were available to him at the time. From a failed Hollywood contract actor, to the host of TVs; "Cavalcade of Stars" -- it was at this point that the mass television audience was introduced to "The Great One", as he was later dubbed by Orson Wells.

I can't explain just how exciting it was to see Reginald Van Gleason saunter onto the set of the Jackie Gleason Show. With his top hat, cape, cane, and mustache he simply took over and launched himself into the middle of some preposterous dilemmas -- usually of his own making. And it was always nothing but laughter as he tried to extract himself from them. This was Gleason's personal favorite role -- and mine too. There were others to choose from as well.

The cameras would push through the swinging doors to close in on the bartender, Joe, as he wiped clean the bar and sang; "They called her frivolous Sal, a peculiar sort of a gal". Joe's only customer every week was "Crazy Guggenhiem" who was portrayed by Frank Fountaine. He spoke with a screwy voice and would always eventually join Joe by singing a duet. Fountaine would then break out into a beautiful baritone voice that was completely inconsistent with the character.

Then, of course, there was the "Poor Soul" whom Gleason portrayed in pantomime. The Poor Soul went haphazardly through life getting the short end of the stick in a tragic comedy fashion.

Finally, there was the king of all comedy, Ralph Kramden, the Brooklyn bus driver, and his eternally patient wife Alice, Audrey Meadows as "The Honeymooners". There were only 39 episodes of The Honeymooners but they are still running to this day. There is a reason, they were great. They were true, nonpolitical, safe, clean family, comedy that could still make people of all ages laugh.

There were other Gleason characters and his personal biography is absolutely fascinating but in the interest of brevity, I want to wrap it up by mentioning some of the other shows that we watched in our house. "The Ed Sullivan show" was a must-see on Sunday nights with everything from Topo Gigio to Father Guido Sarducci and always the important hot entertainer of the night.

Classic TV shows like "The Lone Ranger," "I Love Lucy," "Superman," and "Dragnet" were a big part of many people's childhoods. Whether it was the adventures of cowboys and Indians, the hilarious antics of Lucy and Ricky, or the thrilling escapades of Superman and the crime-solving detectives in "Dragnet," these shows captured our imaginations and entertained us for hours on end.

They hold a special place in our hearts, reminding us of simpler times and the joy of gathering around the TV with family and friends.

## Aunt Katie and Uncle Val

Aunt Katie Moran was my godmother. She was my mother's aunt, my maternal grandmother's sister, a Fenessey. She was married to Valentine Moran and they lived on Valentine Ave. in the Bronx which was located 2 blocks from where we all grew up at 2243 Ryer Ave. I always got a kick out of the fact that Uncle Val lived on Valentine's Ave. A few years ago I learned he was a triplet, but I don't know anything about his siblings. In fact, I have no real memory of Uncle Val other than he was the first person whose wake I went to. We were young children and I remember viewing his body in his casket. It was mysterious and scary but very respectful. As only a child can, I remember that they gave us lots of candy. Aunt Katie on the other hand, I remember well. She was a black dress Irishwoman who was small in demeanor had dark hair in a bun and was always interested in the children. She always made me feel like I was the center of attention. She was just a nice lady. As fate would have it, my school friend and football teammate Gerry DeFabia, lived in their building. Years later at a St Simon Stock neighborhood reunion, I was reminiscing with Gerry and he told me he loved Mrs. Moran. She was always good to the kids in his building. By the way, Gerry was a terrific guy who became a city bus driver and wound up with a family of his living in Edgewater Park by the Throggs Neck Bridge, a neighborhood that became a mini Ryer Ave., Valentine Ave., retirement ghetto. My Aunt Betty Cullinan who was the last family member to live in the neighborhood and who was a bakery worker well into her senior years used to ride the city bus to work. She told me that she met a friend of mine, Gerry DeFabia who used to watch out for her when she rode the Concourse bus. Gerry confirmed this and told me that it looked like I had the market cornered on nice aunts.

Aunt Katie and Uncle Val had two sons John and Sonny who remained lifelong bachelors. They were both good guys who always had time for the children. There were also two girls, Lilian Morgan and Agnes Orff. I honestly have little memory of the girls probably because they got married and left. John and Sonny were there well into my young adulthood. Their apartment overlooked Slattery Park where all the neighborhood kids played and hung out during my entire youth. Young children had monkey bars, seesaws, and swings to play with. The older kids and twenty-somethings had the basketball courts to wear themselves out on. I like to think that they probably spent time sitting at their window trying to pick out the Flynn, Cullinan, and O'Brien kids from the hoard below. We all played there. I suspect the Maher kids remember this park as well because all the visiting back and forth that the families did, they must have played in Slattery as well.

When I was about ten years old I got what turned out to be my first taste of a job. Every Saturday morning I had the assignment of going to the butcher for Aunt Katie and picking up what was always a significant order for her. The butcher was in reality the family butcher because all the women used them. Marvin and Louie were located on Valentine Ave. at approximately 187th Street just one block before Union Hospital where I was born.  I was always greeted by the friendly butchers with a big slice of bologna.  That was the beginning of a lifelong addiction to bologna, yes bologna.  I gave up alcohol 40 years ago, it was a piece of cake.  Bologna, on the other hand, is much more difficult.  Like all the adults I encountered when I was a child, they loved kids.  You rarely found any adults who were any kind of a problem.  I would haul my package to Aunt Katie's and carry it upstairs.  I'm pretty sure they were on the top floor.  I'm not kidding, I was always a big kid and stronger than my friends and I needed it for these butcher runs.  These packages were large.  You wrapped both arms around them and gave it your best effort.  However, this was a labor you would have had to fight me for to take it away.  Aunt Katie would always sit me down when I came into the apartment and give me something.  A cookie, a soda, something.  I always took in the surroundings and savored the smell.  It fascinated me with its earthy scent.  It was strong and overpowering.  It was the smell of the cigars that John always had going and I liked it.  There isn't a woman alive in America today who would put up with this smell but things were very different then.  John would always get a hold of me when I was about to leave the apartment and give me a dollar tip for my butcher run.  When he first did it, I remember being completely taken aback.  When my mother gave us an allowance on Sundays and that wasn't every Sunday, it would be a dime.  You can see why a dollar was so overwhelming.  Sonny was the same way.  We would be playing on the street when John or Sonny would be coming home from work and they would always say hello to us and inevitably give us some change.  We were urchins who didn't know better and would say thank you and run to the candy store.

John and Sonny were simply a few more quality adults we were surrounded by as children. We were blessed to have so many great role models to teach us how to lead fulfilling lives.

# Red Kennedy

John "Red" Kennedy was the first John Kennedy I knew and his life couldn't have been more different than his famous name sakes. "Red", of course, came from his thick head of Irish hair but could have just as easily come from his perpetually flushed complexion.   We were grammar school friends in St. Simon Stock Catholic School in the Fordham section of the Bronx and I don't remember Red never not smiling or laughing. His outgoing demeanor was most deceiving because Red had only come to St. Simon in the seventh grade.  He moved into the neighborhood from the South Bronx and brought with him a toughness that I had not encountered before.

We became friends through sports. Although he was one of the biggest kids on the football team he played full back because he was very fast.  No end sweeps with Red, it was straight ahead run you over football, and this I liked.  As good as he was in football, baseball was his sport. His speed made him a good fielder but his real ability was with his bat.  He went to Cardinal Hayes High School and was a starter on the team.  It seems that Red played in one game at Franky Frisch field on Webster Ave. just north of Fordham Rd. and that the Webster Ave. El ran along the right and center fields of the

124

park. The local legend was that the only player to ever hit one over the El was the famous Rocky Collavito of the Detroit Tigers and New York Yankee fame. Red didn't hit it over the El but he did put one on the tracks. He was a righty and was hitting to the opposite field, this was no small feat.


Red was a barrel-chested bull of average height with broad shoulders and a big friendly freckled Irish face. St. Jerome's parish where he came from was in the later stages of changing from an Irish neighborhood to a Puerto Rican one and conflicts abounded. I remember him telling of how the Puerto Rican kids would chase his pretty older sister Kay after school and of how his father made it clear to him that it was his job to protect her. And protect her he did. Red's cousin Jimmy lived across the Grand Concourse and he told me stories of how Red never debated with any of the kids who were chasing his sister. There was no "you better leave her alone" talk, it was Red catching one of them and immediately going with his fists. Now I know that Jimmy was a fighter because other guys in the neighborhood had seen him in action and he too had moved up from the South Bronx but it was hard for me to see the same thing in Red. He was so damn friendly.

But see it I did. Red, Franky Ford, and I were walking on Valentine Ave. one day when we chanced to meet Billy Myers. The Myers family were "supers" (superintendents) in a building on Ryer Ave. and Billy was a guy with a mean streak. Who knows what was going on in his life to cause such a thing in a young guy but at that stage of my life it was the last thing I would have thought about. I just stayed out of his way because he was prone to violence. This day was different, there was no avoiding Billy. He was older and taller than us and for whatever reason he had some kind of a problem with Franky Ford. Billy was by himself but he started to push Franky around making some kind of demand that has long since faded from my memory. Out of nowhere, no conversation, no posturing, Red grabbed Billy by his hair and pushed him over a small fence into some hedges that were bordering an apartment building. Red had him pinned and jumped on him -- pummeling him with both his fists. In short order, Billy was pleading for mercy. Franky and I pulled Red off of Billy and broke up the fight. Billy was thoroughly humbled and it lasted forever. I never remember him causing any other problem with the younger kids but what stuck out in my mind was the fact that Red never said a word. The friendly bull had an all-business side to him that I admired.

When we graduated from high school, I went to college and Red made his way onto the New York City Transit Police. We would run into each other regularly on weekends at Stack's Bar on Ryer Ave. across the street from the 46th Precinct. More often than not, we would get half drunk and when the night was over I would drive Red home. He lived up the Concourse with his mother and his sister and it was a hassle getting transportation that late at night.

I believe it was a Christmas morning when I went to church and found out the very tragic news that Red had been killed the night before. I was as stunned as possible. I'm sure you have experienced that feeling when someone tells you of the untimely death of someone that was close to you. That first reaction of disbelief and then the need to know exactly all the details of what happened. It seems that Red was at Stacks the night before and had gotten very drunk. An old girlfriend of his had showed up with a new boyfriend and this set Red off. He had no ride home at the end of the evening and went to the subway to get a train up the Concourse. Red, being a TA cop, this would have been a logical thing for him to do. He fell from the subway platform to the tracks and struck his head, killing him.

My thoughts at the time were filled with regrets because if I had been at Stacks I'm sure that I would have driven Red home as I had done on so many other occasions. Of course, I don't have any real guilt over that. Our lives are filled with lots of coincidences and near misses and we accept them for what they are. My thoughts now are filled with regrets for all the alcohol abuse that took place in my life and the lives of so many of my friends including Red. That's behind me and there is nothing that can change all that but I can still today appreciate, forty-five years later, the friendship and good-heartedness of an old boyhood friend.

# Phil the Plumber

Everybody knew him as Phil the Plumber. He was one of several individuals that I have met in my life that I consider a "One of a Kind". If ever there was a knock around guy, he was it. Phil came from Edgemere, New York, located on the Rockaway Beach Barrier Island in New York City. It could be described as an Outer Banks with a Ghetto. The western end of the Rockaways has some very nice middle-class communities but farther east around Edgemere, it is blue-collar, welfare, and forgettable. There have been rumors for as long as I can remember that gambling was going to be approved in the area and that everything would be valuable someday. Right now the things that are of value in Rockaway center around drugs and thieves.

Phil was a rugged guy and had a wiry body that was used to a lot of hard labor. He had jet-black hair that was greying at the temples and very blue eyes. I know women found him attractive because I saw them in action around him in the bars. We met fifty years ago when he was doing work on my brother's house in Breezy Point in the Rockaways. My brother was a fireman and if you know anything about New York City Fireman you know that they're the world's greatest hustlers. He was building this house on a shoestring, doing most of the work himself with help from his friends and his brothers. Phil worked cheap, and this suited my brother. The tradeoff was that he didn't have a plumber's license and when he needed something signed off on he worked off a friend's license. The other part of the tradeoff was that he rarely made it past 11 am before he broke out the Michelobe. When my brother had some money he would pay Phil what he could and always late in the day. Pay him early and he would immediately go to Aqueduct Raceway at a speed that far surpassed anything that he was going to bet on.

I had a sideline in the real estate business and found myself constantly remodeling houses. Phil always got my business and we always seemed to have some kind of deal going on. He was able to do whatever you needed. Carpentry, sheetrock, electricity, heating, and plumbing, just about anything that we encountered in the remodeling work, Phil could do. You had to get used to the fact, however, that a job would never exactly get completely done or necessarily the way you had it planned. Now I must admit that in those years I did a lot of the work along with Phil and he taught me a lot. I also used to drink good in those days and never gave him much of an argument when the Michelob broke out.

Phil was dead on drinking and driving. He wasn't about to give up drinking so he always had a driver. The one that stands out in my mind was Dirty Eddie Albanese. Eddie had a sallow complexion that was probably the result of three packs a day and a day of growth at all times that gave him indeed a dirty appearance. Phil loved Eddie. He abused him and argued with him for at least twenty years but Eddie was an on-and-off public school porter who liked the money and liked to battle back with Phil. Besides, Phil would always make Eddie happy in the end because Eddie had some very laudable traits, a driver's license and he didn't drink. I liked Eddie because he drove Phil crazy and Eddie caused Phil to generate language that would blush an NFL locker room.

I made the mistake once of going shopping with Phil for materials. If you did it once, it wouldn't happen twice. Phil ardently believed that all merchants were trying to screw him at all times. Being the kind of guy who took nothing lying down, invariably he would utter friendly little comments like "You ought to wear a mask when you're robbing people." Now if you're shopping for a shirt at Bloomingdales or perhaps for a fine Beaujolais at a wine store on Madison Ave., a comment of this nature might bring a response of concern from the store clerk. When you threw it out at a plumbing supply or a lumber yard, it ain't quite the same. I heard from Dirty Eddie that they were thrown out of a lumber yard in New Jersey after Phil sounded off. As they were escorted out, the yard workers offered Phil the use of a 2x4 for the ride home. Eddie said it would have been a very uncomfortable ride for Phil if they put it where they suggested they were going to.

I remember one Saturday afternoon we were doing a job on a house in Floral Park, Long Island, and not surprisingly, Phil was late. He eventually showed up and instead of being his usually harried self as he had a propensity to be when he was late, he was relaxed and in very good humor. He had stopped at Davidson's Plumbing Supply in Far Rockaway, his regular supplier, and had found it closed. Now this is unacceptable in the plumbing business. All the suppliers open for at least half a day on Saturday and the plumbers count on this. I would like to answer a question that someone might logically ask at this point. How does a guy like Phil with his wonderful people skills and his fondness for merchants manage to keep a regular supplier? Easy, you find the only Jewish counterman in the plumbing supply business on Long Island at Davidsons. Mort had Phil's number and whatever Phil had to say just rolled off his back. This Saturday was different.  When Phil found the shop closed he went around back and discovered a police car and a couple of cops in the back of the store where they were talking to Morty.  It seems that Morty was held up at gunpoint half an hour earlier and was quite shaken by the unpleasant experience.  At this point, a visibly shaken Morty was happy to see a familiar face, even if it was Phils, and proceeded to relate the details of his harrowing experience.  Phil consoled Morty and joked; "Now you know how I feel! You've been fucking robbing me for years!" Phil was fairly happy the entire day after that.

Tommy Lenahan is an FBI Agent,  as am I, who has been a friend of mine for a long time and who knew  Phil from growing up in Far Rockaway.  At some point in time, we discovered that we had a mutual friend in Phil and Tommy also had a real estate sideline in Long Beach, Long Island where he often hired Phil.  Tommy is one of those guys that if you're his friend he will do anything he can to help you out.  If he doesn't like you, don't bother him. He has a great sense of humor and this combination of humor and shall we say abruptness, I find charming.  I remember Tommy had a supervisor in Queens where he worked by the name of Mike Healy and, to be frank, Healy was universally regarded by the troops as a heartless management drone.  Years later I worked with Healy after he had stepped down from management and I thought he was a nice guy.  It's understood in our job that often otherwise perfectly nice people become flamers when they move into management. Lenahan went into Healy's office one day requesting the upgrading of a dilapidated car that he was driving and Healy sarcastically-responding by writing a note for Lenahan to give to the office car clerk.  The note read, "Please give the bearer of this note one new car." and was signed by Healy. Lenahan saw no humor in this at all and Healy sealed his fate.

Three years later Tommy was at a SWAT training session in Indiantown Gap, Pennsylvania, and was leaving to return home on a rainy Sunday morning. As with most government-sponsored training courses, by the time you get to the end of it, you're more than eager to be on your way and apparently, this was true for the attendees of this one. Tommy was approaching the entrance to the highway and came upon a rear-end collision accident. The accident had just occurred and the driver of the front vehicle was OK but the driver of the vehicle in the rear, Mike Healy, was unhurt but stunned. Tommy called 911 and then attended to the accident. He determined that there were no serious injuries involved although Healy's car had sustained a lot of front-end damage. Tommy spoke to Healy and assured him that help was on the way and that he should just sit tight and everything would be fine. Other agents had gathered around as well. Tommy then reached into his wallet and presented Healy with the note that he had authored several years before. Tommy told him that he hadn't had a chance to use it and that he hoped Mike got the car he asked for. Tommy then drove home and Healy has had to live with this story for years. Don't screw with Tommy Lenahan.

About three years ago Phil's luck ran out. When he was a young guy he had done a lot of work on a military installation in Tuli, New Foundand and a lot of this work consisted of covering pipes with asbestos. This combined with a lifelong smoking habit of a couple of packs of Lucky Strikes a day probably was the cause for a diagnosis of lung cancer. Phil wound up having to go to the VA hospital at Ft. Hamilton, in Brooklyn for radiation treatments. This hospital is a tall building that stands out by itself overlooking the Verrazzano Narrows and Bridge with a spectacular view of New York Harbor. After one trip inside, however, it becomes clear that not a whole lot of the patients are admiring the view. Phil had split up with his second wife at this point and she had moved with the kids to Lake George, New York. They had sold the house and Phil was living like a vagabond catching a couch in friend's places as he could. Tommy came through for

Phil and put him up in a beautiful one-bedroom apartment in one of his houses right on Jamaica Bay in Long Beach. Phil never lived in a better neighborhood.

Tommy, myself, Phi's' brother Eddie, and another friend of Phil, Jimmy Dowling took turns driving Phil to his radiation treatments. Maybe this went on for a couple of months but Phil's condition worsened in relatively short order and he was checked into the hospital. It had been determined that the cancer had spread to both lungs and that there was nothing that the hospital could do but make Phil comfortable. Tommy and I were together in the hospital one afternoon and one of the doctors took us aside and grilled us as to just what our relationship was to Phil. We explained our friendship and this doctor bluntly told us that he would be very surprised if our friend made it through the night. Phil's family was not at the hospital at this point and the doctor now with a compatriot suggested that someone had to let Phil know what the bleak reality was and that in their opinion it should be myself and Tommy. They felt that Phil should have time to see a priest if he wanted to and that there was no real choice. To this day I don't know why the doctors weren't involved in this most difficult task but they weren't, and Tommy and I proceeded to the Intensive Care Unit.

Phil was lying back on the bed which was propped up and he was conscious but lethargic. He knew his circumstances and he knew us. I don't remember who said exactly what but between the two of us we made it clear to Phil that he wasn't getting out of the hospital. We told him what the doctors had said and he acknowledged that he understood. We told him that the hospital wouldn't let him suffer and that we had a priest who was going to see him when we left. We told him to take advantage of the priest and that it was time to go to confession and make peace with God. As we left we met the priest outside of the room and he was an old timer who was all business. We directed him to Phil and a little while later he came out of the

133

room, passed a few cordialities, and was gone. When we went back in Phil was asleep and we left.

Tommy got to the hospital early the next day and went up to Phil's room. Much to his amazement Phil was sitting up in his bed alert and looking relatively well. He admonished Tommy that he didn't think it was very funny that Tommy and I had scared the hell out of him the night before. He told Tommy that he was astonished that we were able to get the priest to go along with this stunt. Tommy was flabbergasted and Phil was dead two days later.

Phil's wake was a Damon Runyon collection of people if ever there was one and by far the most interesting characters to attend were Artie and Lester. Artie and Lester were winos. Now I know that this is a very caustic description to apply to someone but when it comes to Artie and Lester it was right on. Artie and Lester lived in a room above a dry cleaning store in Rockaway. It amounted to a flop house but the owner let them stay there for free because they paid him back with odd jobs but more importantly they provided a presence in the building at night. As with much of Far Rockaway, it was a marginal business in a lousy neighborhood and burglaries were always a problem. Tommy tells the story that he was standing in the lobby of the funeral home when Artie and Lester showed up. Tommy indulges in some very fine suits and is usually the best-dressed person whenever he is in a crowd and is always aware of people's appearances. In stroll, Artie and Lester who were sober, clean-shaven, haircuts, and wearing freshly pressed suits. Tommy said it took him a few minutes to figure out exactly who it was and that the crowd in the lobby had the same reaction. The kidding started and Artie took refuge from the abuse by coming over to Tommy who by anybody's standards was the most respectable person in the building. Tommy started fingering the lapel of the handsome blue blazer that Artie had on. Artie immediately swung open the jacket and displayed the inside where the dry cleaning bill was neatly pinned to the breast pocket of the jacket. Artie beseeched Tommy to go easy on the clothes because he had to get them back to the cleaners the way he found them. Can you imagine?

I always smile inside when I think of this story but I found out later that there was more to it. It seems that Artie and Lester loved Phil for a reason. When Phil was on a roll with cash he would drop by and visit with a case of beer, abuse them for being stew bums, tell them to get a job, and put a twenty in their hands as he left. He was probably their only friend and I think that their tribute to him exhibited by their cleaning up for his wake was more powerful a testimony to Phil than any spoken word at his funeral.

## Tony Bambi

Tony Bambi could have made a good living working in a carnival. Without the benefit of a costume or makeup, Tony had the misfortune of looking like an ape. This is not said to be cruel but rather to be accurate. I could have wasted a couple of paragraphs in the opening of this story by beating around the bush and given a detailed description that would have done the job simply, but not as well as one word; ape. Now, you might think that this is a cruel introduction but actually, it worked very well for Tony. You see, Tony was a member of the New York Mafia and his specialty was gambling and shylocking. Looking like the mean prick that he was came in very useful for Tony.

Tony's real name was Anthony Bambolini and as was the custom with the Organized Crime thugs, it was quickly reduced to Tony Bambi. Tony liked the nickname; hell anything was better than "Bambolini". Bambolini sounded like the name of a magic act and he was glad to get away from it.
When he was fifteen, having concluded his well-rounded education in the Bensonhurst Brooklyn public schools of New York City, he celebrated by getting drunk and going to Coney Island with his friends. During this bender, he thought it would be funny to get a tattoo of the Disney character

"Bambi" on his right forearm. Of course, a tattoo on Tony's forearm made Bambi look like she had a fur coat on. He wasn't called Tony the Ape behind his back for no reason.

Tony finished school and got a job with a family friend in a shipping container repair yard on the Brooklyn docks. He became a full-time welder and a part-time goon. The family friend had some additional businesses that Tony showed interest and ability in -- gambling and shylocking. By the time he was 18, he was collecting payments from deadbeat gamblers and Shylock victims by showing up with a portable propane torch in his hand and reminding them what he did for a living. "I burn shit". Everybody paid.

The Long Island Module boys of the FBI were making a lot of cases out of their non-public office in Levittown, Long Island. The idea came around during the early 1970's, and Joe Fanning was chosen to run it. He was a natural. He was older than the other 10 guys assigned and had the respect of all of them. Most of the agents lived on Long Island and not having to commute to Manhattan alone was an incentive to come up with some good results. This wasn't an issue with this group. It was loaded with self-starters and Jim Abbott, Kenny Giel, and Bobby Levy led the way. There was a talented group of guys to spread the work around to and even the guys who did the least were quite capable when pinned down. If there was an Achilles heel to the group, it was downtime. Even the busiest of squads had a natural ebb and flow with some quiet periods being inevitable. Unfortunately, downtime to these guys meant going to "Potters Pub". Sometimes the gym would win and the boys behaved but other times the boys went to Potters for lunch and inevitably missed dinner at home.

Ken Giel was between marriages, this was the case the whole time the Module existed. Bernie Welsh would announce that they were having a marriage counseling session at Potters for Giel. The party was on. Bernie counseled Kenny to have his teeth straightened. They agreed that this was the root of Kenny's problems. Of course, Kenny had been planning on working on his teeth for years, the straightening had been long planned, and its execution was a coincidence.

Kenny was using the new; "Invisalign" braces that couldn't be readily seen in the patient's mouth. They also couldn't readily be seen in a glass of scotch and water. Kenny got into the habit of dropping the braces into his drink when he was feeling mellow. He was taking a rest from the therapy and this was the best place to keep them aside from their case.

It was the second time that the boys were climbing through the Potters Dempsey Dumpster looking for the valuable invisalign trays when they started to think that maybe their lunches were becoming a problem. They found them both times but announced that Giel was on his own from now on.

The informant was Bobby Levey's, and he told Bob that the bookmaker he was using had a wire room in Manhattan. Bobby had this bettor on the books for a while and he was working on a pay-to-play basis. As long as he kept good info coming in, the cash kept rolling. He supplied a plate number and said the guy's name was Louis and provided a description. Middle-aged, White, 5'10", grey hair and medium build. Boy that narrowed it down. The info was fine and if the plate was right on, a team of three guys would find and surveil him to confirm its accuracy. That's what they did and it was determined that Louis Martin was running a wire room out of the Fox's Lair on Lexington Ave., between 96th and 97th streets in Manhattan. I couldn't think of a better name for the place if you were trying to keep legitimate drinkers out of your bar. In the 70's the east side of Manhattan was the happening singles part of the city and places like Dorians, Hudson's Bay

Inn, Omelia's, Elaine's, and easily a dozen others were competing for the young professionals of the time.

"The Fox's Lair" sounded like a cheater joint, but that would've been a step up in clientele. In reality, it was an old man's shots and beer joint that was barely hanging on. Jimmy Abbott, a natural fit for a shithole bar, went into the Lair and confirmed that Martin appeared to be using the back room for his purposes. He seemed to be the only one in control of the space and the hours he was in the space coincided with bookmaking traditional hours. A wiretap, also known as a Title 111, was applied for and permission was granted to wire-tap the bar. In those days you had to have a location in the immediate area to monitor the wiretap. That's just the way the technology worked.

"A Plant", was secured across the street in an old apartment building. That was good fortune because it also served as a visual monitoring plant for the bar. Usually, background checks were conducted on people that you would approach for the use of space as a plant and in this case, a retired Irish nurse rented the apartment they used. She wasn't living in it at the time but she was paying the rent on it because the rent control was so cheap and she was afraid to let it go. She was a solid citizen who asked no questions and was tickled to get paid rent for the space.

The wiretap was going great. Martin was conducting an illegal betting operation as expected. They kept a shag car in the neighborhood and as people came to the bar to pay or pick up for the week, the shag car would come around and take down the license plate numbers. All was well. An array of bettors and potential testifying witnesses was being amassed. An unusual situation was developing on the wire. Martin was not conducting any calls with anyone about business details of the wire as would have been expected but rather he would leave the bar and go to a pay phone that was located on the corner. If you're under 30, you might be asking; "What's a pay phone?" In the old days, there was no such thing as a wireless telephone. There were no "smart" phones, only dumb phones that had to be connected to a hardwire network. There were telephone company pay phones all over the place. You put your coins in and you got a dial tone and you dialed your number. It was a rotary dial or the more familiar touchpad that was used on the phones and the phones were often inside a glass booth with a sliding door.

Eventually, probable cause was established that Martin was conducting illegal activity on the public phone and another wiretap was secured for this phone. He had let it slip on the wire a couple of times he had to make an important call on the other phone. It proved true that Martin was talking to none other than Tony Bambi on the pay phone and the conversations were about the business of bookmaking. Bingo, this was a score.

They talked about daily handles and problem bettors and a whole bunch of other minutia that were related to the business. It should be noted that the "rules of wiretapping" had a legal requirement called "minimization." In other words, you couldn't simply monitor anybody using the public phone. You had to have someone physically observe the phone booth and confirm that Louis Martin had entered it and was using the phone. Then, you could listen and record a conversation regarding the illegal gambling business. If the conversation veered into other illegal activity, you could keep monitoring and recording. There were some other fine points to minimization but this was the concept.

The wire was a couple of weeks old and it was going better than anyone expected. Every 30 days it was necessary to examine the results of the wire and apply for an extension to continue gathering evidence. An extension wouldn't be a problem. The wire was hot. However, this didn't mean that there weren't periods of boredom. The guys observing from the plant's blacked-out windows noticed that a guy was using the phone booth almost every night around 8:00 pm. He had an Eastside look about him. He was a White guy in jeans dress loafers without socks and a business shirt with rolled-up sleeves. You saw guys like this on weekend mornings at the coffee shops all over the Eastside picking up bagels and copies of the New York Times. His phone call times varied from a few minutes, to as long as 15 minutes. What was this guy up to? Larry Ellis wasn't the best at details. He was a big-picture guy and thought nothing about skipping the bullshit when it came to getting things done.

This minimization shit was a relatively new phenomenon in law enforcement. It was just another defense attorney hurdle that the liberal judges allowed. As far as Larry was concerned, once again justice was being stunted. Now what this had to do with listening in on the next call of the 8:00 mystery man -- I'm not sure. However, Larry thought that justice would be served by finding out what this guy was up to. The call wouldn't be taped, so Larry had a pencil and paper handy to make notes in case this breach of justice uncovered something illegal.

"Hello, Mark? It's Allen. Is it safe to come up?" The caller, "Mr 8:00" (now known as Allen) was talking to an answering machine. "I know you're there and you're not picking up". Allen wondered if this game he played with Mark was worth it. "You know you want me and the asshole is out of town until Friday. Let's do it honey. I can't hold out forever."

"Oh my" wondered Ellis, "What have I latched on to here? Did we get a homo triangle? This might get interesting." A frustrated Allen announced "You know the number. I'm waiting 15 minutes and then I'm leaving and you are going to miss the best humping you have had in years." Allen stood outside the phone booth waited about 15 minutes and then left.

A man of his word, the next night at 8:00 promptly, Allen showed up. Ellis was working and the wire in the Lair was quiet so when Allen went into the phone booth Ellis again monitored the call. It was the same with Allen asking his pal Mark to pick him up with no success, and again Allen was going to wait outside the booth for 15 minutes.

Ellis had two guys working with him in the plant that night and the boys had brought a few beers with them to have with the pizza they brought in for dinner. They were loose, enjoying the evening, and Ellis felt inspired. "Watch this" Ellis proclaimed as he dialed the number of the phone booth. Mr. 8:00, Allen jumped into the booth when he heard the phone ring and listened in.

"Hey, thanks for answering the phone. This is Supervisor Kelly with Manhattan Transit. We're working down below in the subway and we're running some new electric lines. We're trying to get a fix to exactly where we are." Allen responded, "Who did you say you were?"

"Kelly with Manhattan Transit, and we need your help. We know you're in the phone booth and we're trying to get a fix on our location down below in the subway. We just need you to step outside and stomp on the ground three times. We have sensors on the ceiling down here and hopefully, we'll be able to figure out exactly where the phone booth is."

"You can't be serious" replied Allen. "I'm serious as a heart attack. I need your help. Just step outside the booth and stomp three times. We'll read it with our sensors and then we'll know exactly where we are. We appreciate your help." Allen said "This is crazy. OK, hang on."

Allen stepped outside while still holding the receiver in his hand, reached out as far as he could, and stamped on the ground three times. "Did you hear me?" he asked.

"No, I'm sorry we missed it. Please, just one more time. But this time, could you stamp slowly, five times?"

"Good lord, this is ridiculous. OK, hang on." Allen again stepped outside and did as requested, five slow stomps on the concrete sidewalk. "Did you hear me?"

"Yes, we think we got a feint reading. We're getting close. I know it's a pain. Could you do it just *one* more time? This time, take three paces towards the corner and then five slow stamps. We really appreciate it." Allen shook his head and told himself "I can't believe I'm doing this. OK, but this is the *last* time."

Allen dutifully took three paces toward the corner and stamped on the sidewalk five times. A woman walking by held her purse a little tighter and looked at him like he was crazy. "OK, how did that go?" he said.

"That was great! We're almost there. We're pretty sure we have you located. Just one last time, please stomp right outside the booth five times."

"This is fucking crazy. I can't believe I'm doing this" said Allen. There was a pregnant pause and then Allen heard; "You know what, neither can we." It took a moment to sink in and then Allen responded "You dick!" He slammed the handset into the phone and stormed off in anger. The guys in the plant were howling. They couldn't believe that Ellis had done this and that he came up with the idea on the spur of the moment. "Can you believe how many assholes there are in this world?" Ellis spits out through the laughter.

One of the window guys said; "You know, this could be a problem. What if this guy goes to the phone company? Do they know where up on this phone booth? We could get jammed up."

"Fat chance" said Larry. "This guy is going to go to the phone company and tell them that he was waiting for a phone call from his boyfriend when he got a call from the subway?" He had a good point.

Nothing ever did come of the prank but Ellis cemented his reputation as a free spirit to some and a loose cannon to others. The wire was six weeks old and had had one extension. There wouldn't be another. There had been one spin-off case identifying a shylock in Brooklyn but nothing other than that of significance had been determined. They had the evidence they needed for the "Illegal Gambling Business Violation." They would wrap up the monitoring phase of the case at the end of the extension and move on to the overt investigation of the case in the next stage. No one was expecting much to happen and everybody was in a relaxed mode.

The agent in the plant who was keeping an eyeball on the Fox's Lair front door saw a car parking in a meter about six or seven spots up the street. It was 7:00 pm. Nothing unusual there except that the guy who got out and walked toward the bar was none other than the ape-man himself: Tony Bambi. You couldn't miss him. He had a hairy, Neanderthal look that belonged to only one person.

This was a shock. Normally he would have nothing to do with a wire room and there hadn't been any talk of him coming over on the wire. The agent got pictures of him going into the bar and this was useful evidence. Tony was in the bar for about an hour and when he emerged he surprised the guys in the plant by not walking toward his car but rather towards the phone booth. They quickly decided they could legally monitor Tony in the phone booth. As part of the probable cause write-up, he turned out to be one of the people that Louis was expecting to call on this phone.

Most investigations go as planned with a unique wrinkle or two. When Tony picked up the phone in the booth, he blew that rule for this investigation completely out of the water.

"Hey Mark, this is me. If you're there you better pick up. I'm not fucking around." A soft, male voice got on the phone, "Hi Tony. How did you know he wasn't here?"

"I got my sources."

"OK, I'll buzz you in. I missed you."

Tony hung up the phone, went across the street, and entered a high-rise apartment building. They couldn't fucking *believe* it; Tony Bambi was gay! The odds of getting him on a wiretap in such a compromising position were razor-thin. It was simply *incredible*.

A lot of discussion went on as to what to do with this little pearl of information. Should they wind down the wire, sit on any indictments, and use the information to try to roll the ape-man? They had him cold in this case and they were assured that he would be going to prison. Where could a cooperating Tony Bambi take them? A disagreement about what to do ensued.

The United States Attorney's office was eager for the prosecution. No shock there. Most of these guys were in what the agents called defense attorney school while they worked in the USA's office. They learned the trade and moved on to the other side where they could make some real money. They wanted the scalp. A cooperating Bambi could last for years and they would be long gone and get none of the credit. What to do?

A compromise of sorts was reached. This situation went up the ladder in the Bureau to DC where a meeting was held with Justice. It was decided that Bambi would be approached to see if he would roll and at that point, they would determine what they would do. If he rolled they would determine what he could do for them and who he could hand up. If he didn't roll, indict him in the gambling case and send him to prison. Everybody was happy.

The wire was rolled up and the case moved to the next step. Case agent Bill Quinn, renowned for his meticulous approach, laid out a plan contingent on the outcome of the forthcoming Bambi interview. Selecting Bill Flynn and Jim Abbott to conduct the interview showcased his astute judgment. Flynn and Abbott possessed a commanding presence, towering over Bambi with an air of authority that obviated any potential for physical intimidation. Hailing from the streets of New York, they exuded the aura of seasoned law enforcement, their adeptness at engaging in nuanced conversation matched only by their imposing stature. Tony would probably hate them but there was a remote chance he might warm up to these types of guys.

Surveillance showed that Tony had a regular schedule, he spent his afternoons at a ship chandlery business on Clinton Street in Brooklyn. Abbott and Flynn went to visit Tony on an afternoon when the surveillance team determined his presence. When they walked into the office located in the rear of a warehouse building, Tony was sitting at a desk with a guy who looked like a workman seated on a couch beside him.

Abbott took the lead and flashed his badge without identifying himself verbally. He told Tony they had to talk to him and that he would want to have the conversation when he was alone. Bambi picked up quickly and told the worker to wait outside. At that point, the agents identified themselves and got directly to the matter. Flynn started it out with; "Tony we know *all* about your gambling operation." There was nothing subtle about the tactic, it was direct to try to overwhelm him initially. Abbott chimed in that they knew all the players that he associated with and that he was looking at an indictment. Flynn added; "So far this is close to the vest and we're giving you a chance to think about helping yourself." Abbott, as

Flynn began laying out evidence photos on the desk while Abbott said; "You've been wiretapped and photographed Tony, we got you by the balls."

Tony inquired; "How long you guys been following me?" Abbott told him "Months."

Tony examined the photos and said that this didn't mean shit. He wasn't interested in helping the government and he would take his chances. Flynn rebutted; "Tony, what if I told you that we knew about Mark on 96th Street and that there's a good chance that Mark would be testifying in any trial that goes on." He was obviously surprised by this information.

"What do you mean -- you *know* about Mark?"

Flynn replied; "Mark is queer and your hanging around him". "What's that going to look like?"

"You guys are fucking humps" said Tony.

"No Tony, humps would have put this shit out already. We're giving you a chance to bury it," replied Abbott.

Flynn told him that if he cooperated there was a chance he could plea to lesser charges -- depending on how successful they were in any investigation that followed. Flynn knew if Bambi cooperated, a plea was guaranteed -- but you can never say that. You had to keep the carrot dangling for as long as possible. Bambi didn't pause and said he had to talk to his lawyer.

Abbott and Flynn we're glad they had gotten this far before he talked about lawyering up. As Abbott gave him a business card he said; "OK, we understand. Keep in mind, if this goes to trial, you're a well-known guy in this town. You're gonna sell more papers for the Daily News than a front page spread of Charlie's Angels butt-naked." Flynn chimed in "There won't be any secrets."

When Abbott and Flynn left they were feeling pretty good about having planted the seed. Tony getting his lawyer involved was to be expected. What they didn't expect was that Tony never even considered cooperating. They never had a chance. Being gay was the one thing that Tony Bambi would do anything to keep private. Five years in jail was eminently more preferable than being a known homosexual in his world. The one way to ensure that the information about Mark would not come out was to plead guilty. That is exactly what he did.

The case proceeded with his indictment and arrest of all the players involved. Tony pled guilty to a violation of the IGB law and was subsequently sentenced to five years in federal prison. As a Mafia boss, Tony would be untouchable in prison and with his sexual proclivity -- he would have the pick of the litter. In prison, gay sex was somehow acceptable – as long as you were the aggressor. Go figure.

The Module Boys were pleased with the results. While they lost the opportunities that might have accompanied cooperation, they put his operation out of business and the ape-man was off the streets for five years. The Module continued for several years and good cases were developed and prosecuted.

The Federal Bureau of Investigation didn't have "Bureau" as its middle name for no reason. Insiders often referred to it as the Federal Bureaucracy of Investigation. For political reasons that were never really clear, the highly successful Module was eventually disbanded and the Boys went their separate ways to other assignments. They remained friends and Flynn, Abbott, Giel, and Levey worked together on and off on other projects. When they all got together at different FBI functions over the years, the favorite topic of discussion was always the most fun years of their careers, the Module Years.

## Marty and I

Back in my bachelor day's I'd hit the slopes of Killington, Vermont, and the beaches of Hampton Bays, Long Island, with a group of seasoned friends. I may not have been the most adept skier, but I held my own, always cautious to avoid the dreaded black diamond trails. One time I survived by skiing from one spot to another, pausing and picking my way down slowly and carefully for hours. Some of my friends were expert skiers. I knew these guys from my teaching days at Lincoln Hall reform school in Northern Westchester County, NY. That included a guy I truly loved, Frank DeLuise.

Frank's kindness and understanding undoubtedly made every day brighter for me and for the kids at Lincoln Hall. His willingness to meet me at my level, on the slopes or in life, spoke volumes about his character. His presence didn't just improve the atmosphere; it transformed it, infusing it with warmth, camaraderie, and a sense of belonging. Frank's legacy at Lincoln Hall surely lives on in my heart and in the hearts of all who had the privilege of knowing him.

When class let out at 3:00pm, the kids would leave the building at the same street level exit on the way back to their dorms. Frank would post up at the narrow door and every kid who went by would get jabbed, tugged, or manhandled in some way while Frank spouted messages about being good people and doing things the right way. He got me involved in this playful little ritual and we would bounce the kids between us. The ultimate compliment occurred when we found kids coming through the line for a second time. They would run back in the building to come out again because it was so much fun. Sadly, Frank passed away several years ago and is missed and loved by a lot of people.

Another friend from the same ski house was a 'madman' named Marty Listl. Marty and I hung out while we were in our early thirties, single, and in "party mode." We used to drink in Inwood, a famous, Irish-American neighborhood in northern Manhattan. We both worked in Manhattan -- I was an FBI Agent and he was a steam fitter.

Marty was a specimen. He was a 6 foot, 220lb weight lifting power house with "tough" written all over him. In the summer he was a bar bouncer in a very popular Hamptons beach bar where being tough came in handy. However, he could also be a very funny guy. I love Marty but when we got together we were *trouble*. There was an Irish bar on Lexington Ave. named "Mothers." We would meet there on Fridays for lunch and then go on our way. It was popular with both agents and construction workers because it was both cheap and good.

One Friday we had started drinking beer at lunch and just let it keep on rolling. Around 3:00 pm Marty had to go back to the building site he was working on at 79th and Park Ave to wrap up his gear. After that we were both jumping out of work early to go up to Inwood and keep the party going. He talked me into going back to his job site with him to take a tour of the pretty well completed 20+ story building. It was very impressive. We went up to roof to get a great view of Central Park.

Marty, who had no fear of heights, proceeds to jump up on the 4 foot parapet roof wall where he folded his arms like Superman and asked me if I wanted to give it a try. We were over 20 stories high on a roof when this crazy man, who has been drinking with me for hours, is telling me; "if you look down it's really scary."

"Marty listen to me carefully" I said. "I'm going to walk quietly off this roof. I don't want to be a witness where I have to say I saw you fall. I'll see you later." I said this very sincerely – I'll never forget it.

He jumped off the wall laughing and told me to stay and promised he would behave. However, next he suggested that we go over to the water tower where we could safely climb 20 feet to the top for a "spectacular view." Because the tower was on the roof, you could only fall 20 feet in a worst case scenario, and so it somehow made sense to me. I followed him to the top of a water tower on top of a Manhattan high rise, even though I hate heights and had been drinking for three hours with my friend who I knew was a wild man -- and I loved it.

We safely climbed down and it was time to leave the building and head out for Inwood. Leaving the building should have been an easy procedure. There was a construction elevator attached to the building. It looks like scaffolding running up the side and you can see the elevator and all its occupants. They are not automatically controlled. Part of the reason for this is that they can travel at a high rate of speed -- which is a necessary when moving construction personnel and equipment around.

I was ready to get out of there, laughing, and enjoying our antics on the roof when I stepped onto the elevator with Marty. No sooner am I in the elevator when my stomach drops. I'm suddenly stunned and in a complete freefall. Yep, the operator could drop that platform at a free-fall rate of speed for a short distance, and Marty had cued him to do just that. I like roller coasters, but that's because you're expecting it. When it happens unknowingly it's indescribable. It was heart-pounding and terrifying. My fellow occupants laughed hysterically. The ordeal took me a bit to get reoriented. I survived the elevator ride and the rest of our outing and many others that Marty and I had. I often ask myself, how did we survive each other? The madman is a solid family guy who is happily married out in the Hamptons where he is a retired ardent outdoorsman and like me alcohol is no longer a part of his life.

# Breezy Point

My mother and father bought 126 Oceanside in Breezy Point, Queens when I was approximately 15. This was quite a feat for a family that was used to sharing a magic $20 bill with the Mahers. My cousin; Margaret McConnell reminded me of this a while back. We both shared in the money transfer operation that went on between Aunt Mamie and Aunt Bridie. When things got tight I was tasked to run $20 over to Aunt Mamie's and the reverse was true for Margaret. They were each other's safety net.

While it was just a bungalow sitting in the sand still, how could Bridie and Dave have afforded it considering they were $20 away from the precipice at times? Claire Booth Luce, a former Congresswoman and Ambassador had a famous quote, "No good deed goes unpunished". While I believe this is true 95% of the time, my mother, Aunt Mamie, and Uncle Eddie Cullinan managed on one occasion to find the 5%. It seems that they had two cousins; Jimmy and Willy Brennick who were older bachelors. I don't know exactly how they were related but they were American born and in need of care. Jimmy had been a New York cop and Willy had only worked one day his entire life. They lived with their mother in Manhattan. Willy lasted his one day of work at the A&P store and it was best determined that he should stay home and tend to mom. Eventually, mom died and they were living alone. It's my understanding, that Mamie, Bridie, and Eddie took turns looking in on them. I remember when they were healthy; they would come to 2243 Ryer Ave. and visit my mother where they loved to watch baseball on our newly acquired TV. I was fascinated as a kid because they wore high-starch collars with ties and ankle-high shoe boots. Jimmy was a white-haired distinguished-looking man with lots of opinions, while Willy was less impressive and quiet.

It seems that Jimmy had saved some money during his life. He looked to Uncle Eddie at the end of his life for guidance and my mother told me that Uncle Eddie counseled Jimmy to make a will. My mother said Uncle Eddie was careful not to tell Jimmy what to put in his will but rather explained to him that it would be split with the state if he didn't have one. Jimmy listened and consequently, upon his death, he left Mamie, Eddie, and Mom money. As it turned out, he left my mother and father the down payment for Breezy Point.

Jimmy Brennick rewarded the people in his life who were good to him. He changed the lives for the better of my entire family. He couldn't have foreseen all the wonderful years we enjoyed in Breezy Point. Most importantly he provided my mother and father with a retirement home that gave them some of the best years of their lives. Thank you Jimmy Brennick, and may you and Willy continue to rest in peace!

# Gaelic Park

Did my parents miss my after-school activities? Yes, they did -- almost all of them. For the most part, so did all my friend's parents. I played organized football and basketball. Baseball games were pick-up games. Bridie and Dave Flynn were too busy working and taking care of our domestic well-being to consider spending an afternoon or evening at one of my sporting events. It didn't even occur to me that they should be there. However, there was one exception.

It was a school play at St Simoom Stock when I was in the fifth or sixth grade. I had the esteem-building privilege of singing a duet with a girl who I don't remember. We sang "Chisolm Trail" while donning our cowboy and cowgirl outfits. We were memorable and Mom was down in the front row. It was bad enough to sing to an auditorium full of neighborhood people, but adding Mom to the mix made it an ordeal. I'm sure Bridie got more out of it than I did.

It's a very different world nowadays. Kids are transported to and from *all* their activities by a parent or two. I understand the reasoning, but the lack of parental support made me a more independent soul early on.

In 7th and 8th grade I traveled from the Bronx to Manhattan for classes with the Christian Bros. at the Good Shepherd School. I needed the male discipline, but that's another story entirely. Now that I think about it, I was probably acting out because my parents didn't come to my games. I'm just kidding, but I was taking two buses through the New York City boroughs. Safety was not an issue. It *never* was. There were twenty apartments in our building and maybe two or three of them ever locked their door. I liked the independence.

Mom and Dad did come to one game -- and it was a *big* one. It wasn't a championship football game but it was an important one. It was played at Gaelic Park near Manhattan College. The game was played at night and it was under the lights and had a sound system with an announcer. This was a big deal back then.

The Tre-Ford Giants were in the big time. Normally we played all over the Bronx. We played at Harris Field near DeWitt Clinton High School, the Williams bridge Oval, Rice Stadium in the Country Club Section, and Macomb's Dam Field next to Yankee Stadium. The Macomb's Dam field is now the Yankee infield in the new stadium.

The night of the game three Flynn's were playing. "Little" Billy Flynn and "Big" (me) Billy Flynn were on the same team. Eddie Flynn was on the opposing team. This meant that on almost every play there was a Flynn involved and our name was echoed around the stadium all night. I was proud. I have a pretty detailed memory about a lot of things but I can't remember who won the game. We must have because we had a season where we beat everybody and this must have been part of that season. I truly enjoyed Mom and Dad seeing me play. I was a tackle on offense and the middle linebacker on defense. I made a lot of tackles. I was proud and I think they were impressed. Let me end this by saying that what impresses me the most is how well my generation got along often with little or no supervision and how we almost all look back at those times with fond memories. Having my parents at the big game was great but not having them around at most games in another way helped me to achieve an independence of character that has served me well.

## The River Club

The River Club is a posh, private club on the East River at 52 St. in Manhattan. Uncle Tommy Maher worked there as the tennis court attendant and in 1961 when I was 17 years old he got me a job. I was hired as a bellboy/elevator operator and it was an enlightening summer job.

A quick google search states; "The 1932 membership list resonates with the names of the great American families of the late 19th and early 20th centuries: the Astor's, the Roosevelts, the Rockefellers, the Vanderbilt's, the Morgan's, the Pulitzers, and the Graces, among others. The club history estimates that there were "roughly 500 proprietary members, approximately sixty out-of-town members, and about forty junior members, making a total of 600."

This rarefied atmosphere continued into 1961, and some of the members or guests at the time included former presidential candidate Adlai Stephenson, Catholic Superstar Bishop Fulton J Sheehan, and movie actors Gary Cooper and Spencer Tracy.

There were many more but my memory is rusty. The mention of Spencer Tracy reminds me that Uncle Tommy hung around the men's locker room in his downtime with a fellow attendant and friend named "Leo". The two got along famously and shared a common interest, the bottle of Four Roses that Leo kept in his private locker. The two enjoyed a nip now and then and as I recall, Spencer Tracy who took a liking to them also indulged with them on occasion.

The whole experience was enriching for me. I worked with professional bellboys, doormen, bartenders, waiters, and cleaners. We were a diverse crew and I learned to get along with everyone. Of course, being Uncle Tommy's nephew greased the way because everybody loved him. It's funny what stands out from the many things that went on. The elevator was one of these things.

It was the old-style elevator with a traditional sliding door with a sliding, brass, lattice door attached to the elevator. The control was a lever with a knob that the operator used to land the elevator at the floor opening. It was your job to make it even with the floor, it wasn't automatic. If you missed you had to bump it a time or two to make it level, and of course, the passengers were jerked around accordingly. It took me a while but I eventually became an expert at gliding it in. I was very proud of this accomplishment. I could have been a Navy Thunderbird by the end of the summer. I had potential.

The other big thing going on that summer was the magical home run derby conducted by Mickey Mantle and Roger Maris of the New York Yankees. They were referred to in the papers as the M&M boys and chased each other all summer hitting home runs at a record-breaking pace. Eventually, Maris broke Babe Ruth's record with 61 home runs although he played in an extended schedule of more games. Mantle had to pull out of the lineup in Sept because of a hip injury. Poor Maris was greeted with disdain by many fans because he beat the sainted Mickey Mantle.

160

I was hyper-interested in the race of course. I figured out that when I was on elevator duty if I adjusted the glass door going into the restaurant/bar I could see the TV in its reflection from my post at the elevator. The bartenders let me fool with the door because when they were short-handed I would deliver drink orders up to the rooms for them. They were nice guys and would give me a glass of real lemonade now and then. They also introduced me to coffee with real cream. I still love it.

Julia Murphy was the telephone operator. She operated a Lilly Tomlin-style hand plug-in board, located in a booth next to the front door. Julia was probably in her 30s unmarried and full of life. She had a small, silver reflector board that she would put under her chin when she stepped outside the front door. It was the first time I encountered a reflecting board and what getting a tan was all about. Julia was a kick. She was fun. Of course, I was a bellboy in a hotel in Manhattan and I learned other things.

On more than one occasion a well-oiled guest would ask me where the action was. The first time my response was; "Huh?" After a little investigation, the next time my response was; "You're on the wrong side of town pal."

The River Club was a stodgy place, and a prostitute would have lasted about ten minutes. This job at the River Club was a great learning experience, not the least of which was that all jobs can have some dignity. We all worked humble positions at the club but everyone treated each other with respect. I got to witness how popular Uncle Tommy was and the respect he garnered, even though he was the tennis court attendant. I walked away from the River Club with an appreciation for the working man. I never hassled the countless service people and understand that people are just trying to make a living, like that 17-year-old boy many years ago.

## Santa Baby

Years ago the old vintage movie theater in Morehead City, North Carolina brought in a lot of old country western singers and every year had a Christmas variety show. The singers were great. Guys like John Conlee (Rose Color Glasses, Common Man) and Gene Watson (Farewell Party, Paper Rosie) were a few I remember and saw and they were great. Their voices hadn't lost a thing and they filled the 3 or 4 hundred seat theater.

In addition to solo artists throughout the year, a Christmas Show was put on for a couple of weeks as well. It was a throwback, Americana production with a comedian emcee, good female dancers, and an Elvis impersonator. The theater owner had a talented teenage daughter who was a really good singer and was featured along with other assorted acts.

The theater was an old, style theater with a large lobby that led to two aisles on either side of the three-section facility. It held 300-400 seats which descended downward as you went forward towards the full-size stage. This guaranteed everybody a good view. The afternoon we attended the show, we were seated up front, right next to the aisle and steps that lead onto the stage. I needed an easy exit because I always had to make a pit stop at any show I attended.

The show was rolling along and I was enjoying some good old-fashioned Americana at its best. Suddenly, the emcee came to the microphone and said "Ladies and gentlemen it's now that time when I come down into the audience and pick our Santa Claus for the next number!"

"Oh shit!" I thought to myself. It took me ten seconds to realize I was screwed. I'm sitting right by the stairs he has to come down to walk through the audience. I'm Irish, with a big red face, and a white beard. It's Christmas, so I was wearing a red sweater. I'm quite literally the embodiment of Saint Nick. There was zero chance of this guy finding a more appropriate Santa in this entire place, and here I was front and center.

I immediately put my hand up over my face and leaned over towards my wife in an attempt to shield myself. (Fat chance) The emcee walks right by me, and for a moment I thought I dodged the bullet.

That's when I get a tap on my shoulder and I hear this guy whispering in my ear "Let's go big boy, you just saved me a long walk." (Thanks a lot) Before I know it -- he's announcing that he's already found Santa. There was never an opportunity to escape.

Next, I found myself center-stage with a newly acquired Santa hat and a stool. The music starts up and I now have an array of pretty elves dancing around me singing "Santa Baby." My embarrassment quickly turned to fun as I stared at the audience and realized you couldn't see a thing with the stage lights in your eyes.

When it ended, I received a generous round of applause from the audience. I took a bow and happily went back to my seat. It was fun. At the intermission, I went to the lobby where several people greeted Santa and everybody was friendly and laughing. As we made our way home during this pre-IPhone era, Linda and I regretted not having a camera.

# The Ayatollah

In 1979 the Shah of Iran had been overthrown by the Ayatollah Khomeini, a fundamentalist Islamic leader. The Shah had been a longtime ally of the United States who was diagnosed with terminal cancer. After finding shelter in Egypt and Morocco, he had worn out his welcome. In need of first class medical care, he was allowed to come to New York on humanitarian grounds for medical treatment but ultimately was forced to leave the country. For obvious reasons all this was done in as much secrecy as possible.

The Shah flew into LaGuardia airport and was quietly transported to New York Hospital on New York's upper Eastside, where he was ultimately diagnosed as terminal with a short time to live. The Shah was housed in three heavily guarded private rooms with his private security and a detail of FBI agents providing the manpower. There was a real threat of an assignation attempt on his life and this was serious business. Prior to all this happening, Neal Welsh had been recently appointed as the new Assistant Director in Charge (ADIC) of the New York office. The NYO had been a problem child rogue office as far as FBI Headquarters in Washington was concerned. Welsh had been sent in with the mission to get the office back in line with the authority of headquarters. Upon his arrival in New York,

Welsh held a press conference in which he announced his appointment, the nature of his assignment and stated that he was going to take the New York Office apart "Brick by Brick". Needless to say, his pronouncement was not embraced with any joy by the 1200 agents of the office. They felt that his new job title was a perfect fit, A DIC.

The troops responded by having some fun at Welch's expense and bricks were being oddly placed at different locations around the office. In addition the office took to calling Welsh "the Ayatollah" a very unflattering title at the time.

Meanwhile, I was heading up a mobile surveillance group of which we had several. I knew nothing about the Shah being in New York so when I received a call in the middle of the night and was told to round up my team and get to New York Hospital -- you can imagine my surprise.

It seems that the New York press got wind of the Shah in the hospital and it was determined that it was time to move the Shah from the hospital and send him on his way to Mexico. That meant getting him to the Marine terminal at LaGuardia airport -- hopefully without the press figuring it out.

In the course of trying to set up the logistics of the move, things got more complicated quickly. Neal Welsh showed up unannounced at the hospital. The agents outside the Shah's room spotted Welsh and one stage whispered into the agents in the room to "sharpen up, the Ayatollah is coming."

Of course the Shah, who was lucid and alert, had a different vision of which "Ayatollah" was coming. He shot up in his bed, in total fear. "No sir, not *that* Ayatollah! It's just a nickname for our boss. Don't be concerned."

The agents were able to sooth the Shah and his staff quickly. Welsh's entrance actually served to change the subject and I can attest that Welsh didn't learn of his newly generated nickname that night. The Shah was removed safely to Mexico that night and the multiple van subterfuge was greatly assisted with force when the press was kept off the trail by physically blocking their vehicles.

# Martha Jean Goldstein

We have all met hundreds of people during our lives and depending on how old you are maybe thousands. You never know who will be memorable, it just happens. Martha Jean Goldstein has been in the rear of my mind since I met her when I was in high school in 1961. I didn't plan it that way, it just happened.

I spent my Junior and Senior years of high school at LaSalle Academy in what was called; "The Bowery" in lower Manhattan. I received a solid traditional education at LaSalle with the Christian Brothers and the lower east side neighborhood gave me a glimpse of a rougher side of life that existed there in the early sixties. You got panhandled everyday on your way to and from the subway. In addition to my commute from the Bronx, I went to the Houston street station every day and took the D train one stop to Jay Street in Brooklyn where I had an after school job with the Hartford Insurance Company. Gerry Drew, a really good guy and schoolmate of mine, was able to help me get the job since his dad was an executive with the company. The two of us were file clerks from 3:00pm to 6:00pm Monday-Friday.

The Hartford job was my introduction to the real business world and it gave me a positive start in my official work career. Gerry and I were given long index card sized boxes that were filled with what were called "abstracts". I don't really remember what their purpose was, but for three hours a day we sat there alphabetizing them. This was fine and it should have been a long, boring job -- but it rarely was.

As the proud possessors of 17 year-old, raging hormones, our work life was always interesting. A long card table sat at the rear of the room with two girls who were also busy doing the same filing. One of which was a pretty, British damsel in her early twenties. I remember she was very pleasant, married and pregnant most of the time I knew her – but I can't seem to remember her name. The other girl was the unforgettable Martha Jean Goldstein. Now, I'm willing to bet that you have mentally pronounced Martha Jeans last name "Goldstein" as if it rhymed with "Springsteen". It flows, it rhymes, it's commonplace, and it just makes sense. That's a key mistake because Martha Jean would correct *everyone*, *every time* if they pronounced it that way. She would immediately let them know her name was Goldstein (Pronounced like "GoldSTYNE") as in Albert EinSTEIN.

Martha Jean was from Brooklyn and she was a street-smart, 20 year-old chick who was used to bumping up against people and not taking any crap. She was a trim, brunette who wore her hair like Ronnie Spector of the Ronette's. She had a little, bee hive on top and it ran long down her back. Like Ronnie Spector, she wore the Cleopatra eye makeup that made her look like an Egyptian queen. In the vernacular of the time, it could safely be said she had some "big knockers". Martha Jean wasn't downright beautiful but she was had a very sexy way about her.

169

The four of us sat at the long card table with the girls on one side and the boys on the other. We had an immediate supervisor named; "Mac". She was an older woman who was an office fixture. She brought us our work and took care of our time cards. Mac gave me my first glimpse at the fact that the business world is not always on the level when she brought back my first time card for a correction. I had entries that said I arrived at 3:10 pm on a couple of days and Mac asked me what my hours were. I, of course, told her that my hours are 3 to 6pm. She then responded, with a wink, that "life was easier for all involved if my card reflected that". Got it, I certainly wasn't about to rock any boats over this.

Martha Jean also gave me some insight into the fact that the business world isn't always being as 'formal' as I had imagined. She had a playful streak and she loved to distract you from your work. Martha Jean, as I said, was blessed with a sumptuous upper body and she was always posing and waiting to catch you when you couldn't help but take a peek at her. She always wore high heels, and her favorite trick was to take them off and rub my legs with her bare feet under the table. Can you imagine what this did to a seventeen year old, high school boy? She would laugh and ask me why I was blushing. "Don't you feel well? Is everything OK?"

She didn't discriminate; she worked over Gerry as well when she had the chance. The British girl would laugh and say that we were all going to get fired. This type of stuff went on the entire time we worked together, and it likely would have faded from my memory if I hadn't been reacquainted with Martha a couple years after we parted ways at the Hartford.

I was going to Manhattan College located in the Bronx. The name alone should have made me suspicious of the whole experience; "Manhattan

College" being located in the Bronx. During the summers I was very fortunate to work at the "Breezy Point Surf Club" as a cabana boy and bartender. This was a great job. I literally made enough money from tips to pay my entire college tuition bill without taking any loans.

One Friday night I was tending bar at the very popular, main bar of the surf club. It was a big room on the ocean with a large deck and a series of French Doors that were kept open during nice weather. I'd been working my day job as a cabana boy on B court which had about 50 cabanas. A cabana is just a little room with a cold water shower and a place to store beach items. People generally rented them out for the season. This was a very desirable court because it was a more expensive membership area and these members were good tippers. I liked the people and in particular one group of young guys who had named their cabana "The Peppermint Lounge". Of course in the early 1960s, "Joey Dee & The Starliters" headlined at the Peppermint Lounge in Manhattan and this was all very contemporary and "hip". The cabana members typically consisted of firemen, postal workers and Con Ed guys.

One of the guys who hung around this cabana was Pudgy Walsh. Pudgy was a firemen and a famed football coach for both the local semi pro team, The Brooklyn Mariners and the NYFD squad. It was a coincidence that one of the other bartenders that night was my lifelong friend John Corcoran, a fellow Manhattan College trooper. I refer to him a "trooper" because he is the only person who took longer to graduate Manhattan College than I did. (It took me 6 and 1/2 years. It took John 7.) He always quips that his situation was far worse than mine because he started with a full scholarship. Anyway, John was also a defensive back with the Mariners and he knew all the Peppermint Lounge guys very well.

I was working a spot closest to one the doors at the end of the bar when one of the Peppermint Lounge guys named "Fast Eddie" came in and stood near my station. I always thought that the "Fast" came from his way with the ladies. He was a friendly, good looking guy who always seemed to be the center of attention whenever there were women around. However, one day Corcoran told me that Eddie earned the title "fast" because he played end for the Mariners and was in fact extremely fast.

A local band was playing this night and they had just taken a break. We didn't have time to put the juke box on and there was a relative lull in the noise level of the crowd. All of a sudden I heard an unmistakable women's voice screaming at the first open French door entrance on the deck. "You motherfucker, I'm gonna kill you!" The relative lull got, even quieter. "I'll get you, you motherfucker!"

These shrieking oaths were emanating from a soaking wet young lady wearing a t-shirt on top of a two piece bathing suit. By the looks of her, she could have won *any* wet t-shirt contest she cared to enter. As quickly as she appeared, she made her way across the floor and was headed right towards me, or so I thought. She screamed as she moved "Eddie -- you fuck!"

I was still processing all this when I came to a shocking realization; it was Martha Jean Goldstein, in all her glory! Eddie had just entered from the same door moments prior. I could tell that this was going to get ugly and that it was going to happen fast. I jumped over the bar and worked my way over so that I was between Martha Jean and Eddie. I had a lot less ground to cover so she was still on her way over, screaming. John Corcoran, the defensive back was of course a lot faster than me and arrived in a split second. I started calling out "Martha Jean", "Martha Jean" and this got her attention. She stopped when she reached me and had a confused look on her face. I could tell that he recognized me, but couldn't place me -- so I helped her out.

"I'm Billy Flynn, we worked together at the Hartford. You're Martha Jean Goldstein, right?" This was *immediately* met with "It's Goldstein not steen!" She was still digesting this as I began asking her about what happened. "That asshole threw me in the pool!"

John was talking to Eddie and letting him know that it was time for him to leave. Martha Jean told me that Eddie needs to learn how to keep his hands to himself. I was trying to be as soothing as I could. Someone offered her a dry towel and she accepted it and was slowly starting to calm down. In the meantime, John and the head bartender, Dudley Burke were busy coaxing a fast (and drunk) Eddie outside. John enlisted the help of a couple of Peppermint Loungers and they were slowly getting Eddie on his journey back to the cabana. Martha Jean saw him leaving and took it as a personal victory that she had gotten him thrown out -- which was true. She calmed down remarkably well and didn't seem to mind the notoriety that the commotion had gotten her. A couple of her girlfriends appeared and we were able to sit them all at a table and get them a drink. I went back to work and things settled down.

I couldn't help myself, I kept stealing peeks at Martha Jean and her girlfriends -- all seemed well. Eventually, things slowed down and I was able to sneak away from the bar and go over and visit the girls at the table. They were friendly enough and were chatting away with each other giving Martha Jean and I a chance to talk. The music was pretty loud and we were leaning closer to each other in order to be heard. She really was a sexy girl and her Brooklyn tough ways only made her more attractive from my point of view. I was usually a little shy with girls at this point in my life but maybe because of our previous relationship, I was feeling a little more confident and inspired. I kicked my sneakers off and felt under the table until I found Martha Jeans feet. I started rubbing her feet with my foot and slid my foot up her leg. She didn't pull away but she was clearly very surprised. I then asked Martha Jean if she was blushing and if she was OK. She really was at a momentary loss for words. I started laughing and soon she was too. This was too delicious. I reminded her how she tortured me at the Hartford and she reminded me that I loved it, which was true. The kid from the Bronx had just one upped the slick chick from Brooklyn. Life was good.

I of course was interested in seeing Martha Jean again. That night she was with her girlfriends and she went home with them. I called her and tried to get a date but she was reluctant to go. She cited our age difference and her work schedule at the insurance company where she was working in Manhattan at the time. I was of course disappointed. However, I later learned from one of the other cabana boys who grew up in the same neighborhood with Martha Jean that she had a boyfriend and was fully involved. His name was "Fast Eddie".

## More Roast Beef

This is a famous story that had made the rounds of the New York office of the FBI for many years. It was published in a Ron Kessler book and referred to in print elsewhere. The difference is that I have first-hand knowledge of what happened and knew the main player in the story.

Back in the 70's the New York Office (NYO) of the FBI was located at the intersection of 3rd Avenue and 69th Street in a great neighborhood, the east side of Manhattan. A couple of blocks south on 3rd Avenue was a delicatessen that the FBI employees used on a regular basis to buy lunch. Kevin was an agent in the office who had come up through the clerical program to become an agent. Essentially, young people could come into the Bureau out of high school and work in the administrative section while they went to college. Then, upon graduation, they would be given serious consideration to move onto agent training to become Special Agents.

This program produced many fine agents who had a complete understanding of the workings of the Bureau because of their experience. Sometimes, loose-cannons would slip through the cracks. Kevin slipped through the cracks. Kevin thought the best part of the job was a shiny badge and a gun.

One day there was a line in the deli for sandwiches while Kevin waited his turn like everybody else. His turn came and he put his order in. Then, as his sandwich was being crafted, he could see that the sandwich wasn't going the way he had hoped. "Excuse me" he said as he flashed his cherished badge while taping it on the counter; "FBI, *more roast beef*!"

That's right, he *really* said that that. Nick Gianturco was standing in line and witnessed the event. Nick couldn't wait to get back to the office to tell the latest Kevin escapade. The story went around like wild fire and had a lasting legacy. The agents of our era would forever refer to their badges as "roast beefs". You never tinned anyone ever again – instead, you "roast beefed" them. Kevin tried to deny the story but it was to no avail -- he owned it. I guess a no common sense legacy is better than none at all.

# John Kosakowski

John Kosakowski was one of my FBI Agent partners who I worked with in the New York Office of the FBI in the mid-1970s. We did a lot of work together on the Manhattan surveillance squad. John was a great guy, a good agent, and like all my partners throughout my career -- he had a good sense of humor. Most of the good investigators I knew had a sense of humor -- a *dark* sense of humor.

Bill Bradbury, our closest friend, was the Supervisor and I was the Primary Relief. This was a great gig and we all thrived.

Surveillance would range from three to six people – depending on the work required. One person was assigned the responsibility of writing the log for the day's activity. The log would contain a chronological order of all the pertinent observations that the team made. Each individual would then initial whatever entry was relevant to what they saw and could testify to.

My name is William Flynn and my initials are "WF". This is what went on my entries. Everybody else did the same thing. However, John found this out during a pre-trial conference we were having with Asst. United States Atty. Mike Devorkin regarding an upcoming trial.

As we were reviewing some logs that were going to be entered into evidence at the upcoming trial, Devorkin said; "What the fuck is this? Whose initials are these"? I looked at the log and instantly knew they were John's. It seems that John KosaKowsKi had taken to signing his initials as KKK. The initials were somewhat scribbled for the rest of us. We hadn't noticed them before, but the minute you paid a little bit of attention to them, "KKK" jumped out at you.

Devorkin liked John, but he was beside himself. "What the hell was John thinking?" It was clear -- he *wasn't* thinking.

John's defense was that he had only recently started initialing the logs this way and that he thought it looked cool because of the three K's in his name. Apparently, it never entered his mind about the ugly implications affiliated with KKK.

The eventual solution to the problem was to not use John for any testimony or cross-examination. We kidded John forever about his log entries and even Devorkin had some fun with it. This was always the type of ball-busting that kept things entertaining.

Another time John told the story of being assigned to the Albany NY office. He was a newlywed with an infant daughter and his wife was not a happy camper.

They were both from Belleville, NJ where Franky Valli and the Four Seasons started and Mrs. K missed it big time. John had no choice about the assignment and the relationship was struggling. He did his best to make things work, figured his wife would settle in overtime, and the assignment wasn't a forever deal. He assumed within a year or two he'd be able to transfer to the NYC office and they could live in Belleville.

It was a normal work day when John returned home to their apartment at the usual dinner time hour. The minute he stepped in the front door he knew something was strange. The apartment was quiet and his wife didn't respond when he called her name. He called her name again as he proceeded to work his way through the apartment. He became alarmed when it became apparent that his wife and daughter were not home. He drew his gun and cleared every room to make sure no one was lurking in the apartment. As he was cleaning the apartment he noticed items missing and realized his home had been burglarized.

As he began to take inventory of all the missing items he became perplexed."How come they only took *her* stuff?" The baby's crib, furniture, and all her clothes and suitcases are gone. Yep, it was *all* gone, and his wife and daughter had been "taken".

Yep, they were taken all right -- by his wife's father and brother when they showed up with a truck, packed up the whole show and headed back to, Belleville,NJ. So much for Franky Valli, Belleville, NJ and "Big Girls Don't Cry". John retained a relationship with his daughter and was a good father. But it was a troubling time, and a funny story in hindsight.

Years later John's brother, who was a limo driver, was killed in a bad weather accident on route 80 in New Jersey. I remember going to the wake, it was a very sad time. Time passed and John wound up marrying his former sister-in-law. I lost touch with John, but as far as I knew he had a successful second marriage. John and Bill have passed away and I never think of them without smiling.

# Mr. Hoover Never Did Like Them Automatics

Billy Paris was a tall, thin, good-looking guy who hung around the bars on Manhattan's east side. We were Special Agents of the FBI in the mid-1970s. We were single and young women were newly liberated and everybody wanted to have a good time and meet someone nice. It was a Friday night and Billy was getting dressed in his apartment planning to go over to Hudson's Bay Inn on 2nd Avenue. The Bay was a police/agent hangout and on certain nights, single women filled the place.

Billy was the only agent I knew who carried an automatic pistol as an off-duty gun. Everybody carried some form of a revolver and this was encouraged by the management. Billy had a compact Sig Sauer automatic pistol with a clip on the stock that allowed him to slip the flat weapon into the rear of his trouser belt. It was well-concealed and comfortable.

This evening he grabbed the pistol and reached back to the rear of his belt to insert it when the worst possible thing happened. "Bang!" The gun went off. He felt a sting on the cheek of his butt. "Oh shit!" He grabbed a towel and reacted quickly. The towel pressure was controlling the bleeding but his real concern was elsewhere.

He got on his hands and knees and began to examine the floor very closely. He was looking for the slug. He hoped that it had passed through his butt. If that happened, it meant he didn't have to go to the hospital to have it removed. No publicity. He could have a friend clean it up, get an antibiotic, and no one would ever know. Unfortunately, he would have no such luck.

The slug was embedded and he had to take a cab to New York Hospital to get it removed. Billy was tended to by a young nurse at the hospital, a doctor subsequently removed the slug with ease, and Billy hoped this would be the end of it.

When the doctor left, Billy attempted his most charming routine in hopes the report might be written up as some kind of simple bathroom accident. However, the nurse was all business. Gunshot wounds were reported to the NYPD, with no exceptions. This meant that Billy would be on the chopping block facing termination from the bureau. He was doomed.

The call came in at the FBI complaint desk from the duty Sergeant at the 19th precinct of the NYPD. He was confirming the identity of an agent named "Paris" who had been treated at New York Hospital for a self-inflicted gunshot wound. The Sergeant calmed the information immediately. "No, No the agent was fine. He didn't try to harm himself!" The chuckling Sergeant announced; "He shot himself in the ass." And that's the way the story went down. Billy was forever known as the agent who shot himself in the ass. After all, Mr Hoover never did like automatics.

# The Oil Yard

The Berry Bros. oil yard was located on the East River at the very northern tip of Manhattan. It was about 200 yards south of the 225th St Bridge that connects Manhattan to the Bronx. Columbia University's football Baker's Field is located a couple of blocks to the west. The area is generally called Spuyten Duyvil (Spouting Devil or Devils Whirlpool) although Spuyten Duyvil is actually in the Bronx. There is a large C for Columbia painted on the cliff face on the Bronx side of the river. It has been there for as long as I can remember.

The yard was an oil transfer station for oil that was barged into large above-ground holding tanks and then distributed to various small company oil trucks. The customers were the many apartment houses that filled northern Manhattan and the Bronx. The three holding tanks were located right on the river's edge and would send today's EPA into a dither. My father, Dave Flynn was the night watchman for the yard, his second job.

The yard was also located just north of the large 207th St. Subway yard where my father's first job was located as a Track Foreman for the NYC Transit Authority and where he would often end his day. My father was supposed to stay in the little concrete office building overnight and provide both security and access to the pumps for any of the truck drivers who needed oil. I don't know how it evolved but he had some kind of understanding that he could leave the yard late in the evening and go home. He would return at 5:00 am to be available for the early morning drivers.

I remember that there were a couple of junkyard dogs that hung around the property to provide security. Jax and Rags were oil-covered German shepherd mutts and only kids could love them and we all did. There was a junkyard across the street and the dogs wandered back and forth between the two places. A friendly Black man named Elwood ran the junkyard and would come over and have a cup of coffee with my father now and again. I remember Elwood because he was the first hunter I ever encountered. Make that an urban hunter. Alongside the oil part of the yard was an abandoned coal hopper that had preceded the oil business and it was a multi-story black heavy timbered structure that would enhance the scenery of any horror movie. To make it even more onerous, it was home to hundreds of pigeons. Elwood had a refined taste for the city squab and took to hunting them with a BB gun. He took them back to his junkyard estate where he hot-plated them into dinner. Can you imagine?

There were many nights that my father couldn't make it to the oil yard. My older brother David and I were expected to go to the yard and relieve John Manter, the day man. I remember John as an older guy who always looked like he could use a good shower. My mother would always send him a big plate of food on holidays and he was a nice man. I always admired his newer Oldsmobile. My father's cars while always well cared for were older and John's late model Olds was the only new car I encountered among our circle of friends and family. David was the mainstay in filling in for my father but I eventually became old enough to absorb my share of the duty. I would take the bus back and forth from the yard to our apartment in the Bronx but sometimes on a weekend night my friends would drive over and we would play cards and drink beer at our private clubhouse. That of course was when I was older but I remember when we were younger the oil yard was picnic central for the family on weekends. My father had made a long plywood table that we would set up to view the river and he had found an old electric grill along the way. We had hot dogs and played by the water where it was a little cooler in the summers. My parents made the most of it and I know all the cousins came to visit our parties on different occasions.

Actually, during the nice weather, the oil yard became a Sunday hangout spot for the extended family. It was a case of working people making it work. Drinking beer, sitting by the river, and enjoying the fresh air. Life was good, and as all these many years will show, so were we.

## 2243 Ryer Ave

I have an elevator in my house. What does it have to do with Ryer Ave.? Am I showing off? "Yeah, probably." In my coastal tourist beach town of Emerald Isle, NC elevators are becoming pretty common. The big fancy beach rental homes have them installed for both a touch of luxury and to allow the top floor, with the best view, to be the main living area.

When I ride my elevator, I can't begin to tell you how many times I flash back to 2243 Ryer Ave. It is a five-story walk up in the Bronx where we grew up and it came with its own free Cross Fit gym called Stairs. I live my life being grateful and this elevator is just a small reminder for all the good things I have received. Let me tell you more about what our actual building and apartment was like. This won't be the most exciting thing you ever read but if you want to know about a common frame of reference that the senior crowd in our family has, this is a part of it. Most of us grew up in apartment houses. 2243 Ryer Ave was home to two families, the Cullinans and the Flynns. Aunt Betty and Uncle Eddie and their three children, Ellen, Edmond, and John lived in the basement as Supers (Superintendents) and eventually moved up to the third floor. Aunt Bridie and Uncle Dave and their seven children, John, David, Kathleen, William, Patrick, Mary, and Ann lived on the fifth floor which was the top floor. Apartment 18 was our two-bedroom apartment. Jack Flynn had left for the seminary before Ann was born so there were only six children in the apartment for the most part at any time.

Remember now this building was a walk-up, with no elevator. There was a stoop, an interior hallway stairway to the first floor, and four floors with a turnaround set of eight stairs each in between them. My best guesstimate is a total of 76 stairs. Can you imagine looking at 76 stairs every time you went home? How about Aunt Bridie with a brood of kids and an armful of packages tackling that challenge every day? I remember her saying in her old age that she attributed her longevity to the stairs in Ryer Ave. I'm sure there was some truth to that. I remember on Saturday mornings my mother and father would go food shopping at the A&P on the Grand Concourse and we would go down to help them carry up all the food packages from the car to the apartment. We were like ants and I remember the reward was a box of Anne Paige (A&P) glazed donuts for us to fight over when we were done. By the way, we were an exception by having a car. My father had two jobs and his joy in life was his car. When he wanted to get away from it all, he would go downstairs and work on his car. I inherited this from him. I'm always tinkering with my car. I'm forever washing it and rearranging my gear. It's a getaway for me too.

One of the bedrooms was for girls, and one was for boys. When you walked into the apartment you looked straight down a hallway that eventually opened up into two rooms, the dining room and the living room. Immediately, when you stepped into the apartment there was the girl's bedroom on the left and the next door after that was the one and only bathroom. Let me just say it simply. You never used the bathroom without knowing that someone else was probably waiting. To really make it interesting, outside the bathroom door was the hallway which was lined with bookshelves on which the dial-up phone sat. The phone had a long chord that stretched into the bathroom. So, the only way to get privacy in a phone call was to sit in the bathroom. Going to the bathroom in this house was always a challenge.

The next room was the dining room which had primarily a big table and a high-rise bed that slept two. The kitchen was to the left of this room and what made it different from living today was that it had a dumbwaiter. The dumbwaiter was used to remove garbage from the apartments. Uncle Eddie as the Super would pull the roped manual elevator on a certain schedule and eventually put the garbage at the curb for the garbage men to pick up.

As you moved toward the front of the building you came to the living room with a pullout couch. This is where Mom and Dad slept and located off this room was the second bedroom. The living room is where we eventually got a TV and gathered around it in the evening. I remember "The Jackie Gleason Show" and "The Ed Sullivan Show" being my favorites. The living room and the front bedroom had windows that looked out the front of the apartment. The view from the front windows was impressive. The Bronx is a series of hills and the apartment building sat on the top of one of them and there was no tall building facing it to hamper the view. If you looked to the south you could see the Tri-Borough Bridge and straight out you could see across to the East Bronx.

Of course, there was a fire escape attached to one of the windows in the front. As tempting as it was on some of the treacherous, hot, summer nights to sit on it -- this was a 100% no-no. I never saw this rule broken and besides you would have been disrupting my mother's garden. She was a farmer's daughter and all her life there was some kind of plant growing, and the fire escape was her greenhouse.

The girls had the first bedroom and that never changed. The dining room high rise beds and the boy's front bedroom was always subject to change. I don't know what kind of a schedule my mother had but every so often you were reassigned to a new bed and that was that. I don't know when I first heard of the concept that kids had their room but I honestly remember being surprised by it. "Your *own* room? Really?"

My father managed to hook up a clothesline from the kitchen window to the window of the girl's bedroom. He also rigged up a washing machine in the kitchen and my mother's life became a lot less arduous. I can't tell you how many trips I made to the alley between the buildings to pick up a fallen piece of clothing. This was the same alley where homeless men would appear occasionally and start singing a song. My mother and other ladies would wrap a coin in the newspaper, put a clothespin on it, and toss it out for the down-on-his-luck singer. I remember one guy who was a repeat visitor because he came with a ukulele and belted out "Won't you come home Bill Bailey, Won't you come". I cried the whole night long…" In the echo chamber of the alleyway, he truly sounded good.

This top-floor apartment, of course, had the building's black tar roof immediately above its plaster ceiling. In July and August, you could have hatched eggs on some nights. There was a little relief with a couple of fans blowing air around the apartment but not much. Now and then, I remember sneaking out on the roof after dark to try and cool off but the tar was soft under your feet and that didn't last very long. I don't have any, but I know there are a lot of photos floating around of all the kids that were taken on the roof. In particular, it seems to have been a ritual of your first communion to have a roof photo taken.

Marilu Henner, the actress from the TV show "Taxi", has a photographic memory for the days of her life. I never heard of it but apparently, it is a phenomenon that allows her to remember what she was doing on any given day of her life by simply recalling the date. I saw her doing this on TV and I was amazed. I mention this because I kind of have this for some of the artifacts in our old apartment. There is no logic to this but I remember a picture of a bird in a frame composed of real feathers. There was a stand ashtray. Boy would that be a novelty today. There was a full-size mirror in the living room, a standing lamp in the dining room, and a bird cage that we constantly resupplied as the critters perished. There were spoke chairs in the kitchen that we used to flip over and sit in and presto, racing cars. There was the rough plywood closet that my father built in the boy's bedroom and unpainted dressers as well.

The end did come in the mid to late 1970s when my mother and father moved to Breezy Point full-time. It was time to move the furniture from Ryer Ave to Breezy Point and close the door for the last time. I got a hold of four or five of my FBI buddies, a truck and the rainiest day we had had in six months. It rained the entire day and at both ends of the move. My friends were and are great people. They sucked it up and we just did it. By the way, one of my helpers that day was Louie Freeh who went on to become a Federal Judge and eventually the Director of the FBI. It is a nice tribute to the apartment that served us all so well to know that it had at its send-off by a person as important and high quality as Louie Freeh.

# Christmas

Christmas on Ryer Avenue was driven by my sister Kathleen. She created our family traditions and was the one who set the timetable for the different things that we did together. Like everyone else in those days, we would get a *real* tree. Setting it up was a big deal. My father would set the tree up in a stand and that meant that he would take a hand ax and shave the base down so it would fit snug. Making it lie in the stand stable and secure always seemed to take a lot of adjusting -- but he always got it done. This was the beginning.

The lights always came next. They were the tear drop shaped, colored bulbs that some still use today, only bigger. Sometimes we had multi-colored lights that were liquid-filled and bubbled when they were on. They were awesome. I used to sit in front of them and stare. They always fascinated me for some reason. There was always an angel at the top of our tree and the placement had to be just right. My father and my sister went to great lengths to make sure it was perfectly straight.

When this was all done it was time to hang the ornaments. They were made of a fragile, thin glass with wire hooks that hung on the branches. Kathleen directed the whole operation and when the ornaments were completed we had a magic array of color and illumination. We were almost there. The end was in sight and that meant it was time to put the silver tinsel on the tree. Tinsel is thin strips of aluminum made to hang off the branches to give it one more layer of an eye-catching sparkle. This was the most fun for us young kids because we got to throw tinsel around, playfully. We had at it until the packs were gone and Kathleen would straighten out the mess later.

The final touches were the manger and all its figurines. It was a wooden stable with 5 or 6 inch figurines. There was nothing spectacular about it but it added the appropriate spiritual, sacredness to the whole setting. This was challenged by the set of Lionel trains that surrounded everything on the floor. As I write this reminiscing, I'm looking at the trains mounted above a door in my TV room. My brother Pat and I played with these trains endlessly and *only* during Christmas. They were always faithfully packed up and put away for next year. We would place a pill in the stack of the engine and it would puff out simulated clouds of smoke as it rode along. The transformer control allowed you to ring a whistle that sounded remarkably similar to a real train. I never get bored, glancing up and seeing these reminders of those wonderful times.

Midnight mass was an important component of our Irish, catholic holiday season. Not only did I get to stay up late, but the magisterium of the high mass with its elaborate decorations and incense filled the air – it was truly a magical spectacle.

I still have very distinct memories of it all and that warm feeling of togetherness. Scrooge would always on TV and Kathleen made sure we never missed it. That wasn't hard for me and it still isn't. I love the movie. I just watched it on YouTube a couple of days ago. I was awed by it as a child and I still admire the message of hope and joy it delivers at Christmas time. I'm sure everybody has their favorite memories and I hope I triggered some of yours. As Tiny Tim prayed over his family's Christmas meal; "God Bless us everyone."

# Shoes

Do you remember when you were a kid and shoes were a hassle? At least that was the way it was for me. I was always looking around the house to find them. The sock drawer was a "common" drawer and God only knew what you might find in terms of a matching pair. I had low standards for what I considered to be a matching pair. If the colors were close at all, it was a pair. I remember countless occasions when I did my own, little repair on a worn-out pair of shoes. To fix a hole in the sole, I'd cut out a piece of cardboard to fit and go on my merry way. I know I'm not the only one to apply this type of surgery. I suspect most of the older crowd did the same thing. New shoes had to wait a paycheck or two sometimes so you learned to make due.

Linda, my wife, tells me she did the same thing. She recalls kneeling at communion on one occasion and her friends were teasing her for having "Tony the Tiger" in her shoe. She was mortified. Kids can be brutal to each other. But, she got the last laugh. She's not a tiger anymore; she grew up into a human shoe collection.

My Uncle Eddie had a little repair shop in the basement of the apartment building where we lived and often repaired our shoes for us. He would glue flapping soles and put lifts on the heels. We called them taps and thought we were cool.

Uncle Eddie also did haircuts. My brother Pat had light, blond hair when we were eight or nine. I always had a thick, dark mop on my head -- and so by comparison his looked sort of scrawny.

One Saturday afternoon Uncle Eddie and my father were doing a little celebrating and decided that to thicken up Pat's hair they would shave his head. There was an old wives tale that said if you shaved a head the hair would grow back thicker, and so off it came. Pat survived during the day by wearing a little skull cap that my cousin Danny Mason gave him. It looked like a yarmulke and brought along its brand of teasing from the other kids.

Every night my father would come in from his second job at the oil yard and heat a little plate of olive oil. He would then proceed to massage my brother's head. We can't say for sure, but this actually may have worked. Pat ended up with a good head of hair.

Anyways, sneakers were a big deal. Not like the "Air Jordans" of today, but they were a status symbol nonetheless. The elite sneakers of my childhood were Converse. I still hear the old saying today; "You don't slip and slide in the shoes with the stars on the side." Of course, I only got to see them from afar. We were the cheaper, "PF Flier" people all the way. Hang your head and sit on the bench.

I survived and was vindicated when the Duncan Yo-yo guy showed up with PF Fliers on his feet and put on his masterful, yo-yo wizardry show. "Now who's the cool one?"

Another battle I lost was my quest for a pair of Tom McCann Snap Jack shoes. These were the coolest and I *had* to have them. They featured a tongue that snapped into place where the laces would normally be. However, the only tongue that snapped into place in my world was Mom's when she delivered her final; "no". She said if I kept it up the old shoes were going down to Uncle Eddy and he would fix them. There would be no new shoes.

Honestly, I don't remember what I wound up with but it was better than what I had. I told this story to a good buddy of mine and he said he went through the same deal and he never got them either. 60 years later I finally didn't feel so bad.

When we did go buy shoes, it was not unusual to wind up in Alexander's Department Store on Fordham Rd. When you entered the Creston Ave side, you had to walk through the children's shoe department. A salesman would size your foot with what looked like an adjustable Martian boot and bring the shoes to try on. When you settled on a pair of shoes he would take you over to the fluoroscope machine where you stood at a podium and slid your feet into a box at the base. He then turned on what looked like an X-ray machine. My mother and the salesman would look through these special viewers to see your feet inside the shoes and determine if they fit. No problem there. Today, the technicians use similar machines for x-rays and go into another room and wrap you in lead. Add it to the list of the "how did we survive?" I thought that maybe I imagined this machine but I was watching American Restoration one evening and there it was being featured as one of the items on the show.

My mother once told a story about walking to school from the family farm in Ireland. She said a group of children walked to a school three miles away from the hilltop farm they lived on with their shoes around their necks. When they got to school they would put their shoes on. They didn't want to be seen as "bumpkins" without shoes, but they also knew that they had to preserve the shoes as best they could. The shoes came off for the walk home. They also knew there could be a long spell before it was time for a new pair.

This common sense frugality served my mother and father well throughout their lives and spread to their children. The reward for our humble beginnings stays with me every day. I live in circumstances that few people would be unhappy with. I have more shoes than I will ever need and I appreciate every good thing that I have in my life.

# Randy

Randy Hebert is a good friend I read to each week. He's a retired Marine Corp Major who contracted ALS/Lou Gehrig's disease in the mid to late 1990s. In 1999 I began this tradition and I continue to do so to this day. Randy has defied the odds. It's rare a person survives ALS this long.

My wife Linda and I moved to Emerald Isle in January 1996. I had been transferred to Camp Lejeune, NC where I spent my last three years with the FBI before retiring in November 1998. This was my first experience with the Marine Corps and I loved it. They were three fun years as an investigator and I walked away with a deep respect for the Corp and the many Marines I've met.

It was at this point when George McLaughlin, a retired Marine friend of mine, approached me and asked me if I would be interested in helping him read to a marine named Randy Hebert who had ALS. I mentioned this to Linda and she pointed out that we had seen this young guy and his pretty wife on TV testifying in Congressional hearings. Randy spoke with great difficulty and Kim translated for him. We were impressed at the time.

George explained the circumstances regarding Randy and I said I would. I went with George to observe and later on my own to take over for

George. I was now reading to Randy a day a week for an hour and the setting was pretty formal. At different times Randy has had other gentlemen who have also read with him but several of them have passed away and I am the only one reading now.

Kim was and is the most gracious person you would ever want to meet. She immediately made me feel welcome and at home with the Hebert's. When I read to Randy there is always a nurse in full time attendance and over the years there have been many women who have had this job. The nurses communicate with Randy by sounding out the alphabet and arriving at a letter when Randy moves his eyes. He is unable to move any other part of his body. They eventually carve out words and sentences and despite how arduous this sounds, they are amazingly patient and it isn't quite as cumbersome as it sounds. I on the other hand have tried this and move at a snail's pace. There have been other more sophisticated computer-related techniques involving eye movement but they did not work out for Randy.

Randy has been blessed with very professional help who more often than not wind up friends of the family. In the beginning; it was pretty straightforward, I would show up say hello to everybody, read for an hour, and move on. Over the years this has evolved into something quite different but the ice breaker occurred when Randy had an eye condition that was causing his eyes to close involuntarily.

I'm naturally a kidder and when this happened one day, I suggested to Randy that things were getting bad when I began putting him to sleep. He immediately responded, via the nurse, that of course that was not the case and the nurse explained his condition to me. However, he understood what I was doing and we both had a good laugh over it. He is able to display a slight grin, and this is how I realized Randy had a good sense of humor.

Karma evened things out and my turn came when I was tired one afternoon and couldn't keep my eyes open. I fell asleep while reading -- right in the middle of a sentence. The book fell right out of my hands and hit the floor, with a 'thud'. I looked up and there was Randy greeting me with the biggest grimace smile that he could muster shining right across the room. I started laughing and our bond was formed. I knew Randy was one of the boys and we could kid each other as we saw fit.

Our reading sessions are generally conducted in his driveway or at the beach. Those who know Randy know that he is a supreme sun worshipper. Randy was a very good-looking fit sun worshipper in his prime. After years of dealing with this "ravishing" disease, he looks better than 90% of the people I know. We never have a session without discussing the depth of Randy's tan. I on the other hand am under an umbrella the whole time. I like the sun but I had a serious melanoma on my back several years ago and do my best to stay out of it.

What happens in the driveway is that people will stop by constantly and we will have regular chat sessions. I discovered over time that these little meetings are far more important than the reading itself. Randy is a social man and he enjoys talking to people and watching people interact with one another. As a result of all our little pow-wows the hour has stretched out over the years to a couple of hours. I enjoy this as much as Randy does.

One year on Randy's birthday, Kim had people stop by the driveway and give Randy each the same present, a bottle of his favorite sun tan lotion. When I left, there were two dozen bottles or in Randy's world, one summer's supply. By this time I had come to view my sessions with Randy as an important part of my life.

My job is to help break the monotony that Randy's disease has confined him to. I have made a conscious decision to make sure that my sessions are positive, upbeat experiences. The nurses on duty, as well as Kim, have become an important part of these sessions. I like to chat and discuss our lives because it allows us to take breaks from reading.

Currently, I have been reading on Saturdays and I always show up with a little spiel about what is going on with me and Randy frequently will ask me about what I think about politics or something topical in the news. I always kid and am fond of saying, that all interruptions are welcome. I'll always ask Kim and the nurse on duty what's happening in their lives.

Another treasure trove of conversation when she comes around is Kim's sister Dale. She is charming, and a natural comedian. As I always say, reading is what happens around here when we run out of things to talk about.

After many years of reading to Randy, I realized that they had home videos made of him and the family before he became ill. Kim set it up so that we could watch them one afternoon and I don't know what I was expecting but after I saw them I was blown away. Randy was nothing like the image that I had created in my mind. While I knew that he was a fun guy who was a heartthrob in the neighborhood when he was single, I arrived at a more sedate image of him in my head.

Randy is a serious Christian husband and father and participates totally in everything that goes on in his family. Dennis Del Mauro, a retired Marine Corps Colonel friend of mine, knew Randy in passing when Randy was assigned to the General's staff and he told me that Randy was on the unofficial list of those headed somewhere. This added to my mental picture.

In the home videos, the thing that immediately caught my attention was Randy's speech. I had never heard him speak and here was this young guy with a Southern accent. Of course, he has a Southern accent, he's from the South. He was playful and teasing throughout the videos, but why wouldn't he be? The videos were of the family on different holidays when everybody was laughing and having a good time.

Randy was in excellent shape and he and Kim as a couple could have been decorating the top of a wedding cake. All these things are good and reinforced my observations about the wonderful family I came to know.

They also confirmed that I was right about Randy, years before I knew he had a good sense of humor.

I have also had the pleasure of watching Randy's kids grow up. It's a regular habit for Nicole and Kyle to kiss their father when they come into the room. They love their father and I have never heard anything but positive things about their careers and social lives. They are both accomplished and a tribute to totally attentive parents. Kim Hebert could not have been a better wife for Randy to have. She is remarkable in the way she has handled what would have been catastrophic for a lesser person.

We have read a lot of books and my favorite is one of our earliest books; "Into Thin Air" by John Krakauer. The book was a best seller about a disastrous climbing season on Mt. Everest where many lives were lost. Reading an exciting book to Randy has helped to stretch out our sessions as well. When I think I'm done for a session, I often look forward to seeing how long the next chapter is and inevitably say "One more?" Randy has never refused. I take it as a nice compliment.

Sometimes I naturally know I'm in synch with Randy. We were reading "John Adams" by David McCullough and it was a bestseller. I was struggling with it. It was more about John Adams than I ever wanted to know and I finally suggested to Randy the possibility of bagging it. I don't think we ever tossed in a book before that, it was the first time. It took him as long as it took to communicate with the nurse to agree. We have moved on from a couple of other books over the years. We don't spend enough time together and it seems like a waste to struggle with a book we are not enjoying.

We read a book about Tom Watson's caddy who had ALS. Tom Watson was, of course, a famous golfer and his caddy Bruce Edwards wrote a book, "Caddy For Life" about his ALS struggle. The book showed the true class of Tom Watson who absorbed all costs associated with Bruce's disease and who took care of his family. What stood out in the book was the reference to someone in California, I believe, who had ALS for about twenty-five years. This turned into a kidding point between Randy and me about how he was going to kick this guy's butt. I've told him on occasion to get started on my eulogy. It takes a while to get words down but there was no doubt he would have to give one.

Randy is a competitive Marine with a phenomenal memory and most importantly a fierce will to live. I remember Randy saying he is driven by a desire to see his children grow up. I'm sure if I addressed the subject now he would say he is waiting for grandchildren.

At one point we read Mitch Albom's book "Tuesday's With Morrie". The book was about Albom reconnecting with his former teacher, Morrie Schwartz, and how Schwartz was dealing with his ALS disease. He met with Morrie on 14 Tuesdays while he interviewed him for the book. Schwartz was able to speak during this process. Ironically, at this time, I was reading to Randy on Tuesdays.

In the book, it is indicated that Schwartz no longer practiced Judaism but was rather an agnostic. This was more striking to me than anything else written in the book. This was in direct conflict with what Randy believed.

Randy was once interviewed by Men's Health Magazine, and the young lady who wrote the story asked an insightful question. "What is the first thing you think of when you wake up?" I know what my answer would be; "Why am I still here?" Not Randy, he responded; "Thank You Jesus for another day". Wow. That blew me away. This man has figured out a way to be grateful for a condition that no one I know could endure.

Randy Hebert is living a productive worthwhile life under the worst of circumstances. Randy is a Christian and draws his strength from his belief in Christ. I am a man of struggling faith and my association with Randy has helped me progress in my journey -- another benefit I have gleaned from reading with Randy.

You can't talk about Randy without talking about Kim. She is a force of nature. Kim is one of those people who sees no barriers that can't be overcome if she decides to do something.

She ran ALS walks in town for many years. I'm not sure but maybe there were four or five walks. She was assisted by Kelly Rogers a girlfriend of hers whose previous husband, Ryan White, had contracted ALS around the same time as Randy. He passed away after several years with the disease.

These walks were huge successes and only ended because they were too draining on the girls to keep up. Randy has nurse coverage all day and Kim is able to take the time to take care of herself and household needs as well as squeeze in odd part time horticultural jobs. Kim is Randy's nurse throughout their evenings.

Kim has a green thumb and the grounds of their home are like a botanical gardens. What free time she has is spent gardening. They have expanded their home and Randy, with the assistance of his dad Lloyd, designed the improvements. Randy assisted the contractor by shopping for a lot of the materials. He would arduously work with the nurses to get down on paper all the information they needed to shop. I have run into him in the aisle at the local Lowes store shopping just like anyone else. It is truly amazing how Kim and Randy get stuff done and handle it in the normal course of business.

Kim can describe the early years of Randy's disease and the battles with Congress to get full coverage for other military victims of the disease. She stepped up with others and fought the fight to get it done. This was no small accomplishment and a testimony to her and Randy's grit.

I have talked with friends of mine over the years of course about Randy and his disease. It often comes down to; "What would you do if you were confronted with this disease?"

I have heard that when you are unable to eat anymore, you are confronted with the decision to have a feeding tube installed or not. At this point, you can refuse and you will hasten your death. I don't know if this happens or not. I have never discussed this with Randy or Kim. I know my friends would choose as early death as possible to escape the disease. At my age 80, it would probably not get that far but if it did I would not extend my life. Even though I have been a witness to the most extraordinary battle with this disease and see that a fruitful life can still be lived, I'm not Randy Hebert. I would allow my life to end.

My wife Linda and I consider Randy and Kim as our dearest friends and we have socialized together on various occasions. I'm reading to Randy until he buries me like the other readers. Just kidding, a little macabre cop humor is something we both enjoy. I love my friend and will take this road to wherever it leads. As Randy says at the end of every session; "Love you man."

# The Lottery

My younger brother Pat and I were FBI Agents. We both retired and sadly Pat passed away in 2012. During the 1980's Pat lived in Marathon, Florida in the middle of the famed Keys. The keys are magnificent. Strips of islands connected as far as the eyes can see. Pat used to say "You better like to drink or fish or you will lose your mind in six months."

My wife Linda and I, along with several other friends, would often vacation in Marathon and it was party time. Pat was a character. He liked to have a good time and shot from the hip. He liked bars. Strangely, I never saw him drunk. I don't think he ever had more than two glasses of wine in an evening. He enjoyed hanging out in some of the upscale marina bars but he also knew where the fisherman bars were and he had a lot of friends who were fringe characters in town. They all knew he was an FBI Agent, but they knew he was closed mouth. They were comfortable around him and they would talk.

It was this ability of Pat's that brought him into contact with a young guy one night who shared an interesting story. He told Pat that he won the Illinois lottery -- 28 million dollars. Pat said he had no reason not to believe him. He asked the guy how that worked out for him and was told; "not too well." Initially, the notoriety of being the big winner made him feel special and he enjoyed the attention. The kid said that he bought eight of his friends Harley-Davidson so that they could all ride together. In less than two years all but one of his friends sold their bikes for cash. They always had a good reason to sell but he felt betrayed.

The young guy said that he bought his sister a house. She was delighted. About a year after he bought the house, she began complaining that she needed new furniture. He said the implication was clear -- buy me some new furniture.

The kid said that whenever he went out partying, all his friends assumed he was picking up the tab. At first, he did pick up the tab and he felt like a big shot. Then he noticed that his friends were buying other people drinks and putting them on his tab. He was feeling disrespected. The kid said that there was a never-ending list of people who were hitting up for money and that he felt guilty if he didn't say yes. Everybody knew he was loaded but he felt angry with himself when he said yes to people he didn't want to give money to. But he didn't want people talking about him not being a good guy and doing the right thing.

Pat asked him how his friends and family relationships held up under the stress of all this. The kid said they didn't hold up. He no longer had contact with his family and most of his friends were gone. Meanwhile, while telling the story he told Pat that he was an exception, mainly because Pat was with the FBI, older, and he felt comfortable. Generally, he didn't bring up anything about his winning the lottery. He felt like people couldn't help themselves and that on some level they ultimately would be jealous of his good fortune. The kid said the whole experience made him very suspicious of people. He had a girlfriend, it took him a long time to trust her.

The kid's analysis in the end was that he felt that people had the attitude that since he was young and won the money and hadn't earned it, he had an obligation to spread it around. He told Pat if he had it to do over he would have tried to keep his good fortune as quiet as possible.

Pat concurred and bought the couple a drink to make a point that not everybody wants his money. He told them how much he enjoyed their story and wished them well as he headed home knowing he had a great story to share.

# Green Peace

One morning back in the early 80's, I was driving my usual route to Manhattan, over the lower level of the George Washington Bridge. On a typical day, rush hour would add about half an hour to my commute. But, this morning the traffic was moving exceptionally slowly, and soon barely crawling along.

I was listening to WINS radio station which was a local news, weather, and traffic network. I quickly learned that today's cause of the traffic congestion belonged to an environmental activist group; "Green Peace". On this particular day, they were attempting to win over the public via an extreme "save the planet" demonstration which involved suspending a man from the lower level of the bridge in a wheelchair. (You can imagine what kind of mess had been created from this stroke of genius)

Eventually, I managed to creep up to the scene of the action where there was a Port Authority uniformed cop standing alongside the single lane all traffic had been funneled into. I rolled down my passenger side window and pulled out my badge and "roast-beefed" him, before screaming; "Cut the fucking rope!"

The officer looked at me with a big smile and said; "That makes you, number five!" he replied as we both started laughing. He then stuck his head into my window and said; "Can you believe these fucking assholes? The moment we rolled up on this thing – that was the first thing we *all* said. Just cut the fucking rope!'" We laughed again as I rolled away -- knowing I had another great story for my list.

# Sean Hannity

I am very proud to say that Sean Hannity is my cousin. Sean's mother Lillian was my first cousin. My father Dave Flynn and Sean's maternal grandfather Cornelius (Connie) Flynn were brothers who emigrated from Ireland as teenagers in the 1920's to New York. Sean is 17 years younger than me and I didn't see him much as a kid.

The Flynn side of my family didn't stay in touch as much as my mother's side the Cullinane's and Maher's did. I was aware that Sean was a burgeoning young Conservative radio star in the making and during the early 90's when he was in Atlanta I had an FBI buddy of mine, Rick Barry, make me a cassette tape of part of his radio show. I heard it and loved it.

Sean came to New York in 1996 as I was about to spend the last three years of my FBI career at Camp Lejeune in Jacksonville, NC. Our paths crossed briefly in New York where I went to his radio show one afternoon with my wife Linda and Sean's sister Teddy, a delightful human being. Like Sean I was a radio junkie as a kid. I was hooked on rock and roll while he followed talk show hosts. However, in North Carolina, I became an even bigger fan of both his radio and Fox Cable TV shows. I was hooked. Even if I wasn't related I would have been a big follower of his. We think alike.

Years later, I was listening to the radio show one day when I nearly came out of my shoes. Sean was talking about being pro-law enforcement and acknowledged that he had several law enforcement members in his family. He mentioned two of his cousins from the Bronx who became FBI agents. My younger brother Pat was also an agent who sadly passed away in 2012. Sean went on to proclaim that as he grew up we were considered to be the "deity" in his family. I was truly taken aback. You have to understand that when circumstances are appropriate, I occasionally tell people that Sean Hannity was my cousin and the reaction is typically; "Oh wow, that's cool." Here he was calling me "deity" on air to millions of people, I regaled in the honor.

Over time Sean repeated the reference to his FBI cousins and one day on impulse, I picked up my phone and called his show. I got through rather quickly. The screener did a little due diligence to verify that I was indeed Sean's cousin before returning and telling me to "hang on -- I was next up". It was a little surreal. I was in my living room and on impulse I wound on the phone 15 minutes later with Sean Hannity, the biggest radio show host in the country, talking to millions of listeners. I was glad it happened so quickly. I didn't have enough time to get too nervous. Like testifying, once I heard myself speaking my nervousness subsided. We had a nice chat about family and I took my opportunity to unveil the FBI for the politically corrupt organization it has degenerated into since I was an active agent.

I stayed in touch with Sean, texting him very sparingly, but enjoying our friendship. He graciously invited my wife and me to visit him the next time we were in New York. We eventually took him up on his offer but Sean's sister Teddy and my sister Mary turned it into a bit of a family reunion. I'm glad they did. We met at Del Fresco's restaurant across from the Fox studio in Manhattan. We were a group of about 30 to 40 people seated in a banquet room when Sean came in from his radio show. As he walked into the room, he apologized for being a little late but said "Who cares, I don't know any of you anyway". It was funny because it was true.

The group consisted of my brother, sisters, their children, and their spouses, Teddy and her family. We settled in and we went around the room and everyone introduced themselves. We all bantered back and forth with each other -- it was a lot of fun. Of course, the ever-generous Sean picked up the hefty tab.

After the restaurant reunion, we all ventured across the street where we filed into the FOX TV studio and watched Sean's live show. His in-studio guests were Lara Trump, Gregg Jarrett, and Lawrence Jones. Lawrence stole the show when he came over to where we were all sitting and made it a point to shake everyone's hand.

When the show ended, Sean graciously hung around and posed for photographs. He and Teddy could not have been more accommodating and the family was thrilled.

Sean finally moved to Florida a few years later, a threat that he had been making on air for years. I visited him and had dinner with him at his new home recently. Linda and I typically spend our winter months at our condo in Vero Beach, so it was a quick drive. It was eye-opening to see his work ethic. The man is a disciplined machine. The radio and TV show relentlessly require daily attention and Sean's rigorous martial arts training makes for a full, daily schedule. He is the workhorse of Conservatism in this country. He gets the necessary repetitive message out every day about how the left has deserted its traditional liberal positions and has fallen headlong into anti-American hateful progressivism. I bless you, Sean, for all you do, and I'm forever proud of our relationship.

Did I tell you this one?

# Danny Boy

No book I would write would be complete without me telling you about Danny Griffin. When I met my beautiful wife Linda she was a single mom with a ten-year-old son, Danny. When we married we became a new family and Danny boy, as he was affectionately known in the family, was a young teenager. Sadly he was killed in an accident at age 15 and our lives were forever indelibly changed. He has never been forgotten. He was a sweet boy with the same thick, dark hair, and a million-dollar smile as his mother. He was a part of our lives for far too short a period.

My sister Kathleen had two young girls Ellen and Kathleen who would come to visit and they were fascinated by the young teenage boy. Of course, they were, his room with records and posters and all else that a teenager would have. I mention this because Danny entertained these girls for hours on end. No matter where he went they followed and he was always cheerful with them. There was no end to his patience. In reflection, I'm not surprised because Dann Boy was a beautiful person. He was a good-natured kid without the proverbial mean bone in his body. With his passing, I can't begin to describe the profound sadness it brought to Linda and all of us who loved him. I pray every day that we will be reunited and I always remember the million-dollar smile.

Did I tell you this one?

Did I tell you this one?

## About the Author

Bill Flynn is a Bronx-born and raised, red-blooded American. He's a retired, FBI Special Agent who now resides in the serene coastal region of Carteret County, NC with his beautiful wife Linda. Raised in the vibrant tapestry of Irish culture, Bill inherited the tradition of storytelling from his ancestors. His tales, a blend of wit and wisdom, weave together the fabric of his colorful career and everyday encounters. Some anecdotes are mere snippets, evoking laughter with their brevity, while others unfold into essay-length reflections, offering moments of pause and contemplation. Within these narratives lies a treasure trove of experiences that Bill invites you to explore, laugh along with, and perhaps find a bit of yourself in.

Did I tell you this one?

Did I tell you this one?

Did I tell you this one?

Did I tell you this one?

Did I tell you this one?

Did I tell you this one?

Did I tell you this one?

Did I tell you this one?

Did I tell you this one?

Did I tell you this one?

Did I tell you this one?

Did I tell you this one?

Did I tell you this one?

Did I tell you this one?

Did I tell you this one?

Did I tell you this one?

Did I tell you this one?

Did I tell you this one?

Did I tell you this one?

Did I tell you this one?

Did I tell you this one?

Did I tell you this one?

238

Did I tell you this one?

Did I tell you this one?

Did I tell you this one?

Did I tell you this one?

Did I tell you this one?